Seeing the WHITE BUFFALO

Robert B. Pickering

Denver Museum of Natural History

DENVER MUSEUM OF NATURAL HISTORY PRESS

DENVER

JOHNSON BOOKS

BOULDER

Published in the United States by Denver Museum of Natural History Press, 2001 Colorado Boulevard, Denver, Colorado 80205, and Johnson Books, a division of Johnson Publishing Company, 1880 South 57th Court, Boulder, Colorado 80301.

9 8 7 6 5 4 3 2 1

Published in cooperation with the Denver Museum of
Natural History:
    Designer: Kay F. Herndon
    Managing Editor: James T. Alton
    Photo Editor: Nancy Jenkins
    Assistant Photo Editor: Jennifer Ehrlich
    Publications Manager: Heidi M. Lumberg

    Editor: Suzanne Venino
    Proofreader: Laurie Rogers

Library of Congress Cataloging-in-Publication Data

Pickering, Robert B.
  Seeing the white buffalo / Robert B. Pickering.
    p.   cm.
  Includes bibliographical references and index.
  ISBN 1-55566-181-5 (cloth: alk. paper).—ISBN 1-55566-182-3
  (paper: alk. paper)
    1. Indian mythology—North America. 2. Indians of North America—Great Plains—Religion. 3. Teton mythology. 4. American bison. 5. Bison—Social aspects. 6. West (U.S.)—Social life and customs. I. Title.
E98.R3P52   1997
299.72—dc21   97-7411
                                                     CIP

Printed in the United States by
Johnson Printing
1880 South 57th Court
Boulder, Colorado 80301

 Printed on recycled paper with soy ink

To Dave and Val Heider,
for your help, humor, and openness

CONTENTS

PREFACE

I spotted the story in *The Denver Post*. On August 20, 1994, a pure white buffalo calf had been born on a small farm in Wisconsin. I was aware of the significance of the white buffalo to numerous Indian tribes; it was considered sacred and had been revered by Plains Indians for centuries. Told and retold through generations, the story of White Buffalo Woman prophesied that she would return to Indian peoples in times of need. The birth of a female white buffalo was a rare and portentous event.

I finished my morning tea and called Karen Sekich, executive director of the American Bison Association, to see what she knew. Karen and I had been working together to develop an exhibit on the American bison for the Denver Museum of Natural History, where I am curator of anthropology. She had already spoken with the Heiders, the owners of the herd, and knew many of the details. Her conversation with the Heiders, however, was different from most calls from people claiming the birth of a white buffalo, which, if authentic, would be a highly valued—and valuable—animal.

Karen receives several calls a month from people inquiring about white buffalo calves, and when she explains that blood tests are necessary to verify that a calf's coloring is not the result of crossbreeding with white or light-colored breeds of cattle, the callers rarely follow through. Yet when she explained the blood-testing requirement to Dave Heider, he wanted more information on the procedure and inquired how much it would cost. Karen realized that the Heiders were unaware of the importance of the white buffalo to American Indians. That would soon change.

In the days and weeks that followed the birth of the white buffalo, the story was reported in newspapers across the nation, broadcast on the evening news, and translated into numerous languages as it made worldwide headlines. I, too, joined in the media circus when Karen suggested that I travel to Wisconsin to see the newborn calf and write an article or two for *Bison World*, the magazine of the American Bison Association. She would provide me with an introduction to the Heiders, and the Association would help cover my expenses.

With no more thought or expectations than that, I started down a path that has introduced me to many fascinating people, revealed surprising aspects of Indian spirituality, and eventually led me to write this book. I have no doubt that this work will lead to other encounters, stories, and projects. Sometimes, when looking back on choices made, people have second thoughts. In this case, I can truly say that if I had the chance to do it all over again, I would.

I flew to Milwaukee in mid-September, just a few weeks after the birth of the white buffalo. My time there would be brief, as I had only two days to meet the Heiders, arrange an interview, see the calf, take pictures, and head back to Denver. The hassle of getting out of the airport was more annoying than usual. There was a delay at the car rental counter—the computer was down. The employees tried their best, but with the long line of customers, it didn't look good. By the time I was finally behind the wheel and traveling west to the Heiders' farm in Janesville, Wisconsin, the blue skies had turned dark. I watched the sky grow darker still as I listened to the weather report on the radio. There was a thunderstorm warning calling for heavy rains, high winds, and possibly golf ball–size hail. Looking through the windshield, I didn't need the radio to tell me what those black thunderheads meant. As the announcer listed the towns included in the bulletin, I smiled. I would pass through them on my way to Janesville. The storm and I were headed in the same direction.

It hit while I was still on the highway. The heavy, threatening clouds let loose with a pounding rain and a fierce wind that nearly blew me off the road. I could hardly see past the windshield. Other cars had pulled off to the side, yet for some reason I kept going. I wondered if the storm was an omen, or maybe a trial to see if I was worthy of seeing the calf. Such thoughts were irrational, I knew, certainly beneath the consideration of a scientist such as myself, but then so was driving in this outrageous storm. If this was a quest, I wanted to be worthy, so I kept going.

Finally the storm broke and the sky began to clear. A patch of blue started to grow beyond the dark and bilious cloud bank. In this clearing, puffy white clouds now reflected the sun, looking majestic and luminescent, the kind of light that Albert Bierstadt captured in his paintings of the western landscape, showing both power and serenity at the same time. The white clouds seemed to form a buffalo—a white buffalo—or so I convinced myself. The dark storm clouds appeared to be a wild, rampaging herd of buffalo surrounding a peaceful, white calf. Sometimes you see familiar shapes in the clouds, sometimes your mind plays tricks on you, sometimes you just don't know. Even scientists fantasize.

As I drove on, a flock of Canada geese flew overhead. Could this be an omen too? Then a pheasant appeared along the side of the road, running in the same direction that I was headed. What did this mean? I looked for signs and omens in the landscape. Maybe I was looking too hard. Why, I wondered, am I traveling more than a thousand miles to see a curious little buffalo calf? Has something important happened here? Or is this simply a natural oddity that has captured the public's attention?

There are many ways to view the phenomenon of the white buffalo calf. In this book I have chosen to examine it from four perspectives: from the personal perspective of the Heiders, whose lives are forever changed by this event; from the historical and cultural perspective of American Indians; from the biological perspective of the anomaly of a white buffalo;

and from a spiritual perspective, the meaning that others look for and find in such an event.

Both before and since my visit to the Heiders' farm, many people have traveled to Janesville to see the white buffalo, and each one probably sees something different. I hope that this book will help you look at the white buffalo from different perspectives. What you see is up to you.

ACKNOWLEDGMENTS

The creation of any book requires many hands to make it happen. Betsy Armstrong, former manager of the Publications Program at the Denver Museum of Natural History, initially encouraged me to write this book and helped guide the project through its formative stages. Stephen Topping at Johnson Books and James Alton at the Museum then saw the project through to completion. Kathy Honda, Kathie Gully, and Dorothea Miller pulled together library resources to add historical detail to the story, and Suzanne Venino polished the manuscript. I thank all of you for your help and support.

The cooperation of and hours of interviews with Floyd Hand, Arval Looking Horse, and John and Virgene Tarnesse made it possible to share their views on the white buffalo. They are all extraordinary people with whom I look forward to spending many more hours in the future. A special thanks to Father Peter Powell of the St. Augustine's Center in Chicago for his kindness and guidance.

I owe a great debt of gratitude to Karen Sekich, former Executive Director of the American Bison Association. She persuaded me to go to Wisconsin and meet the Heiders in order to write several articles for *Bison World,* the association's bimonthly magazine. Those articles evolved into chapters, which evolved into this book. Similarly, Todd Runestad, former editor of the Denver Museum of Natural History's *Museum Quarterly,* persuaded me to write for the general public rather than limit the book to an academic audience.

To Brian Ward, Susan Maas, and Paul Jonjak—members of the National Bison Association and my mentors in learning about many aspects of bison ranching—I gratefully thank you for all of your help. I have become an enthusiastic supporter of the bison ranching movement, only hampered in my pursuit of becoming a rancher through lack of money, land, and experience.

To the Shirek family, Doug Paulson, Mr. and Mrs. Harold Berry, and Gerald Parsons, DVM, I thank you for your patience and for answering my many questions. Your cooperation will benefit bison enthusiasts long into the future.

Finally, Dave and Val Heider deserve my most heartfelt thanks. On only the strength of a phone call, they welcomed me to their farm and shared many hours of conversation, funny stories, and personal experiences. They reviewed my transcripts for accuracy and put me in contact with people integral to this story.

This book was born through the help of many willing and enthusiastic people. Any errors that may have inadvertently crept in, however, are entirely my own.

CHAPTER ONE

SEEING A
SMALL MIRACLE

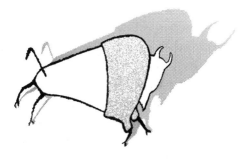

Dave Heider first saw the calf early in the morning. He and his wife, Val, run a small herd of buffalo, fewer than twenty animals, on their farm in southern Wisconsin. Part of the buffalo pasture is wooded, and during the previous night the herd had settled in among the trees. Approaching the buffalo, Dave saw that one of the cows had given birth, and a newborn calf huddled next to its mother. The calf appeared light in color and at first Dave thought it was an optical illusion, a play of light from the sun filtering through the trees. Then he saw that the baby buffalo was completely white. How unusual, he thought, and on closer inspection he found it more unusual still. The calf (Color Plates 5 and 6), a female, had a brown nose and brown eyes, not the telltale pink nose and eyes of an albino.

News of the white calf spread quickly through the small farming community of Janesville, population 3,198, and a photo appeared in the local paper. The story was picked up by regional newspapers as well. It was a newsworthy event, to be sure, but little did the Heiders know just how much so.

Within twenty-four hours of publication of the photo, the Heiders had their first Indian visitor. He told them that he had just come from a Sun Dance. At these sacred gatherings—ritual ceremonies that involve fasting, purification, and dancing as the Indians reaffirm their relationship with the powers of creation—the participants often have visions. The Indian standing on the Heiders' front porch had had a vision of a white buffalo calf, and now he had come to see the calf, the one pictured in the newspaper. This was Dave and Val's first clue that their little white calf was more than an oddity of nature.

In the days and weeks that followed, the Heiders would learn of the powerful spiritual significance that the white buffalo holds in American Indian culture. The Indian tribes of the Great Plains revere the spirit of the white buffalo—its hide, horns, and skull have sacred uses in Indian medicine and religion. Stories regarding the white buffalo are important in Plains Indians' oral traditions handed down through the centuries. Many Indian stories have long since faded from memory as tribal elders and traditional story-tellers passed on. One story that survived is that of the White Buffalo Woman.

Details of the White Buffalo Woman story vary from version to version, but the common theme among all of them is the close relationship between the Indian and the buffalo. The story tells of how the buffalo nation, offering themselves as a source of food and sustenance to their human brothers, assist the Indians with continued survival. The story ends with the promise that the White Buffalo Woman will return to the tribes in times of need. Some Plains Indians consider the return of the White Buffalo Woman as comparable to the second coming of Christ. Could the little white buffalo calf born on an August night in the Heiders' pasture be the fulfillment of this prophecy? It was this possibility that excited the Indian community.

Since the first news report, the interest of the mass media, along with that of both Indian and non-Indian visitors, was overwhelming. Everyone wanted

Miracle was born in late summer of 1994. With her white coat, and dark eyes and muzzle, she has become the focus of worldwide attention as the fulfillment of the prophecy of White Buffalo Woman. (© DMNH/ Robert B. Pickering)

to see the white calf. Native Americans came to see the animal promised in prophecy. Many non-Indians came to see if something spiritual was taking place. Others just wanted to see what all the fuss was about. The Heiders named the calf "Miracle."

Within two weeks after Miracle's birth, the Heiders were getting hundreds of visitors every day. They had to barricade their driveway and post signs to keep the cars off their own and their neighbors' lawns. Too many people were coming for Val and Dave to accompany everyone up to the buffalo pasture, and they were not about to let total strangers go traipsing around the farm by themselves.

As is typical in midwestern farming communities, family and friends pitched in to help. Val's parents and sister volunteered to take people up to the pasture. A nephew took photographs of the calf, and each visitor who signed the registry book could take a copy along with a one-page fact sheet about Miracle. With so many people, and farmwork still to be done, Val had little time to cook, and more than once Mrs. Beckman, the Heiders' sixty-nine-year-old neighbor, brought dinner over for the family. Another neighbor mowed their lawn, and still another made signs telling people where to park and warning visitors not to venture into the buffalo pasture. Not everyone understood that buffalo, sacred or not, are still wild animals.

▲▰▲▰▲

Just as Val Heider had predicted, I had no trouble spotting their farm. Cars were parked along both sides of the road. Val's sister, Vickie, and her mother, Doris, answered my knock on the front door. They were slightly reserved at first, which wasn't surprising considering that hundreds of strangers had been coming to the house. I had spoken to Doris by phone the day before, and when I introduced myself, her greeting warmed considerably. She asked me to sign the guest book and have a seat on a lawn chair. The weather was still hot in mid-September, and Vickie offered me a tall glass of cold water from the farm's artesian well.

We chatted about all the hoopla surrounding the calf and the crowds of people who had come to the farm. Vickie said it probably wasn't a good day to try to interview Val or Dave. The extraordinary attention of the press and the public in the past few weeks had overwhelmed them, and the whole family was stressed because of all the publicity. They were a bit stunned by what was happening.

Vickie offered to take me to see Miracle, and we walked about fifty yards from the house to the fenced-in pasture. No one goes to see the calf without an escort. A half dozen people were already there, along with Val's father, Jerry, who was answering questions. Behind the fence, next to her dark, shaggy mother, stood the small white buffalo.

I don't know what I expected to see when I first saw Miracle. Part of me expected to look into eyes that were knowing and wise—maybe even a sign of recognition that Miracle knew why I was there. Another part of me expected just a normal little calf. Looking quite delicate standing next to her large, dark mother, Miracle was about the size of a sheep and nearly the same color. If Miracle knew she was special, she didn't show it. She looked pretty normal to me.

A healthy, spunky little calf, Miracle weighed about forty-five pounds at birth. Although her coloring obviously set her apart from the rest of the herd, none of the other buffalo paid any special attention to her. Now, after nearly a month of constant scrutiny, both mother and calf appeared wary of people. It was difficult to take Miracle's picture because her mother kept leading her away.

Buffalo are highly intelligent animals, and Miracle's mother seemed to know that the focus of attention was on her calf. During the first month, the dam vocalized almost constantly to Miracle, much more than she had to her first calf, according to the Heiders. And though Miracle's mother was the dominant cow in the herd, she stayed toward the back of the herd and positioned herself between the calf and the growing audience. This protectiveness is common defensive behavior for many animals, particularly large herd animals whose young make vulnerable prey. Distinguishing between dangerous predators and people with cameras would tax the mothering skills of most buffalo cows.

I struck up a conversation with Jerry, Val's father. He was formal at first, but after we discussed the weather, livestock, and the farm—standard topics of conversation in rural communities—he loosened up some and we hit it off. He reminded me of the neighbors and townspeople I had known while growing up on the rolling prairie of southern Illinois. As a long-time Midwesterner who had recently moved to Colorado, I felt very much at home on the Heiders' farm.

An Indian man and his blonde wife stood near the fence as well. I recognized him as being from the Denver area. He was one of the Aztec dancers who had performed during a major exhibition on the Aztecs at the Denver Museum of Natural History, where I work. He didn't know me but said he knew my boss and my boss's boss. I guess I knew my place.

After a short while, I walked back to the house and joined Doris and Vickie, sitting around a picnic table. The Aztec dancer and his wife were there too. Doris introduced us all to Val. The Aztec man sat

Dave and Val Heider—the Janesville, Wisconsin, couple on whose farm Miracle was born. For the last two years they have coped with amazing changes in their lives while still managing to maintain both balance and a sense of humor. (© DMNH/Robert B. Pickering)

down beside Val and started talking about himself and the importance of the calf. I stayed in the background and listened. My conversation could wait; I wanted to hear what he had to say.

He told Val that he was Aztec and represented a quarter of a million Native Americans in Mexico. The news of the white buffalo already had traveled through Mexico to the Indians of South America. They had been waiting for this event. The calf was sacred, he said, and people would come from around the world to pay homage. His wife, a freelance writer from Sweden, was planning to write a story about Miracle for some Swedish publications. The calf would likely bring wealth, he claimed. People would send donations of money, lots of money, maybe a million dollars or more. Others would try to exploit the calf, he said, and he asked Val not to let them. He spoke of practical matters as well, of tax breaks and of the need for security and crowd control. Val's eyes grew in astonishment. Was she really hearing all this: security, crowd control, a million dollars?

Before the birth of Miracle, the Heiders had lived a pretty normal life—Dave driving heavy trucks for the Rock County Highway Department and Val running her own office-cleaning business and also working for J&B Janitorial Service. By their own description, the Heiders are hobby farmers. They raise a few beef cattle and occasionally board horses. Chickens, ducks, and geese have the run of the place. In 1990, they decided to add some bison and bought three heifers at an auction, including Miracle's dam. A few months later they purchased a bull, Marvin, Miracle's sire. At the time of Miracle's birth, the Heiders had a herd of fourteen bison.

Just twenty-four acres, the Heiders' farm is nestled between a slow-flowing stream flanked by massive cottonwoods and a rolling hillside shaded by oaks. It's a small but active operation. Some of the outbuildings look as if they were built more out of necessity than planning. On the day of my visit, it was pleasantly quiet except for the cicadas in the trees, the cows in the next pasture, and the sound of a lawn mower in the distance—typical summer sounds in rural Wisconsin. A field of hay had recently been cut and the smell of sweet clover hung heavy in the humid air. Two small, friendly calico kittens and a gray tabby played in the yard. Norman Rockwell would have been comfortable here.

Dave pulled up in his pickup truck and parked in the yard. I had seen him earlier but had decided not to intrude. He had looked preoccupied and his demeanor had indicated that he didn't want to be bothered. Dave came over to where we were sitting around the picnic table and took a seat on the riding lawn mower. He had just returned from one of his many errands. Dressed in a T-shirt and work pants, he looked tanned and muscular, clearly a man who gets his exercise at work, not at the health club. He listened to our conversation but kept his thoughts to himself. He appeared tense, his jaw muscles tight. He wasn't frowning, but he wasn't smiling either. Again, I decided it was not the time to introduce myself. That was probably a good decision because Dave quickly moved off to take care of some other business.

It was getting on toward four o'clock, and about a half dozen people were waiting to be escorted to the pasture to see Miracle. Val agreed to take them, and I went along. When we reached the pasture, other people were already lined up along the fence, different people than I had seen earlier. Again, Val's father, the local expert, answered questions. An artist with palette and easel was painting a huge four-by-six-foot canvas of Miracle and her mother, his homage to the pair. Tiny medicine bags hung on the fence (Color Plate 13), tied there by people leaving offerings to the white buffalo calf. Some of the visitors talked in quiet, almost reverent voices. A young Indian woman and a boy walked silently up to the fence. I wanted to ask what tribe they were from and what they thought of the white buffalo calf, but I felt uncomfortable interviewing strangers and refrained. A reporter from National Public Radio wasn't so shy. Seeing a good angle, he zeroed right in on the Indians. He interviewed several other Native Americans gathered at the fence and also talked to Val.

I overheard a woman say that she was from Chicago, that she had been to the Mayo Clinic for medical tests and had decided to come see the calf on her way home. People from all walks of life were there— young, old, rich, poor, Indian, and non-Indian. All wanted to see Miracle. A slight man with a reddish beard stood off by himself. He was conservatively dressed in a short-sleeved shirt and tie and, if I'd had to guess, I'd have pegged him for a small-town Methodist minister. He told Val he had put all the money he was carrying in the donation can. Val just looked at him, incredulous at this reaction to Miracle.

Val and I finally had a chance to talk while standing at the fence. She agreed that it wasn't a good time to interview Dave. Tomorrow, first thing in the morning would probably be better, she said, when—she hoped—things would be a little quieter and less hectic. I told her about my background and my work as curator of anthropology at the Denver Museum of Natural History, where I was heading a team that was putting together a major exhibition entitled *The Great American Buffalo.* The exhibition would cover almost everything relating to buffalo, from their place in the prairie ecosystem to their importance in Plains Indians' culture to modern bison ranching. The white buffalo and its spiritual significance to Native Americans are an integral part of that story, and we wanted to include it in the exhibition. The contacts I had made while working on the exhibition had led me to this pasture in Wisconsin to write an article on Miracle for the American Bison Association.

Although not a member of the association, Dave had called the ABA shortly after the calf was born to ask if it was rare. The ABA's reaction was cautious, said Val, almost chilly. The association explained that blood tests—for the calf, the dam, and the sire—would be necessary to determine the calf's bison lineage. I explained to Val that the ABA receives a number of calls each month from people claiming the birth of a white calf. The tests are to authenticate that the calf is not a cross between a bison and a white breed of cattle, such as Charolais. With most calls to the ABA, if the people go through with the blood test at all, the calf in question turns out to be a bison-Charolais cross. Val looked surprised that someone would try to fake something like that.

Just about every aspect of recent events had taken the Heiders by surprise—the birth of the white calf, the Indian prophecy that the calf was sacred, the newspaper stories, the TV broadcasts, the worldwide headlines, and all the people who had come to see the calf. Much had changed in their lives in a little less than a month's time. But what had really caught their attention was a prediction made by Floyd Hand, a Lakota elder who had come to see them just a few days after the white calf's birth.

Floyd Hand had traveled from the Pine Ridge Reservation in South Dakota to Wisconsin because he had had a vision and felt it was important that he come in person to tell the Heiders. A man with a powerful presence, Hand told Dave and Val about the prophecy of White Buffalo Woman. The Heiders were slightly awed but also a little dubious of holy men, wherever they came from. Hand then told them of his vision: The calf's sire "would lay down his life for the calf." Hand had seen a large obstruction in the bull's intestines. The bull was going to die. On September 1, just twelve days after the calf was born, the bull died during the morning hours.

A local veterinarian was called to conduct a postmortem on Marvin, the bull. The vet found a large blood clot in Marvin's stomach. The results of the postmortem certainly seemed to confirm Floyd Hand's prediction. Was this coincidence or was his vision verified? Perhaps even more than the birth of the white calf, the death of Marvin—and Hand's prophetic vision of it—unnerved the Heiders.

There was just so much to absorb, even if they couldn't comprehend it all. And throughout all of this, the people kept coming. And they called, and they wrote. During the first few months, the telephone rang about every three minutes, sometimes until eleven o'clock at night. While I was interviewing the Heiders, a man from England called to offer his congratulations and a donation of money.

People sent letters asking for photographs, information—anything. Artists requested photographs from which to paint pictures. Entrepreneurs sent samples of merchandise they wanted to market. Although most of the people who contacted the Heiders were seeking spiritual meaning, others were simply looking for a new product line.

Because of all the interest, the Heiders found themselves facing major and unexpected expenses, everything from upgrading the fencing around the pasture to putting in portable toilets. Numerous offers were made to buy the calf, even the entire herd. Various Indian tribes wanted Miracle for religious reasons. Rock star Ted Nugent, who had written a song about the white buffalo, contacted the Heiders about buying the calf. From circuses to corporate buffalo ranchers, the offers came in.

The Heiders decided to keep Miracle. From the beginning, even before they understood the full significance of the white buffalo calf, Dave and Val had felt a genuine responsibility to make sure that Miracle received proper care, that she not be exploited, and that all people would have access to see her. The opportunities and challenges of the next two years would test their decision.

CHAPTER TWO

A HISTORICAL PERSPECTIVE

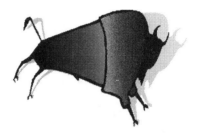

Lakota legend says that in early times, there were no buffalo on the plains. Then one day, buffalo emerged from the earth. The Lakota, who were too small and too weak to kill the buffalo, were always hungry. The buffalo, with a wisdom greater than that of humans, saw the hardship of the people and took pity on them. First Buffalo said, "My tribe and I will come back to you in great multitudes. Use us well, for one day, we will go back into the earth again. And when we have gone, the Indians will be no more."

The myth of the origin of the buffalo is common to all of the tribes who have lived on the Great Plains: the Lakota and other bands of Sioux Indians, as well as the Cheyenne, Crow, Blackfoot, Apache, Comanche, Arapaho, Pawnee, Kiowa, Mandan, Hidatsa, and many other peoples. The story differs in detail from tribe to tribe, and even within tribes. Some versions claim that the buffalo emerged from a lake, while others claim that they emerged from a cave or from the inside of a mountain. Yet, all the stories symbolize the close bond between humans and buffalo, a relationship based on mutual trust and obligation. The buffalo nation would let the humans eat their meat, wear their hides, and use their bones for tools, and in return the people had to be respectful of the buffalo and to honor them in appropriate ways.

The people hunted buffalo and their families grew. But sometimes the people fought and killed each other, for they did not know how to live properly. They did not know the proper ceremonies and rituals to honor the buffalo nation. At times the buffalo herds were not to be found and many people died of starvation. During such a time, the Lakota were visited by Pte San Win, the White Buffalo Woman (Color Plate 2). According to legend, she taught the Lakota how to live properly and instructed them in the necessary rituals. She presented them with a sacred pipe, and she promised to return in times of need.

The story that follows is an abbreviated version of the myth as told by Archie Lame Deer, a Sioux medicine man from the Rosebud Indian Reservation in South Dakota.

WHITE BUFFALO WOMAN

A long time ago, before the time that people remember today, the seven sacred council fires of the Lakota came together. The sun shone all the time and there should have been game but there was none, and the people were starving. Two young men set out on foot to look for game. This was the time before the people had horses. For a long time, the two young men did not find anything. They then climbed a hill to get a better view of the land. Far in the distance they could see a being coming toward them. They knew it was holy —wakan — *because it floated rather than walked.*

As the being came closer, the young men could see that it was a maiden, more beautiful than they had ever seen before. She wore white buckskin that shone brightly in the sun. Her dress was decorated with marvelous quillwork of sacred designs, in radiant colors that no ordinary woman could have made. The holy one was White Buffalo Woman. She carried a large bundle and a fan of sage leaves. Her eyes revealed great power.

The two young men were awed by her beauty. One of the young men had evil thoughts, and wanting to possess her, reached out his hand. Being very holy, she could not be disrespected. The brash young man was instantly struck by lightning. Only a few charred bones were left where he had been standing.

The other young man had acted honorably. White Buffalo Woman told him to return to his people and tell them that she was coming to their nation and that she carried a message from the buffalo nation. The young man ran back to his camp and told the chief what had happened. The chief sent the crier through the camp, announcing for everyone to prepare for the coming of the sacred one. They raised the big medicine tipi. After four days, they saw her coming toward their camp. She carried a large bundle before her.

The chief invited her to enter the medicine lodge. White Buffalo Woman entered and circled the interior in the direction that the sun turns. She made an altar with a buffalo skull and instructed the people on the proper rituals. She opened her bundle and gave to the people the chanunpa, *the sacred pipe, and she taught them how to smoke the pipe and care for it. The smoke rising from the bowl was the living breath of the great Grandfather Mystery, she told them. She showed the people how to use the pipe in prayer, and the right words and gestures.*

"With this holy pipe," she said, "you will walk like a living prayer. With your feet resting upon the earth and the pipestem reaching into the sky, your body forms a living bridge between the Sacred Beneath and the Sacred Above. The Wakan Tanka *[Great Spirit] smiles upon us, because now we are as one: earth, sky, all living things, the two-legged, the four-legged, the winged ones, the trees, the grasses. Together with the people they are all related, one family." She taught the people how to be holy and to live as part of the living world.*

White Buffalo Woman spoke to the women of the tribe, telling them it was the work of their hands and the fruit of their bodies that kept the people alive. "You are from mother earth, and what you are doing is as great as what the warriors do." She opened her sacred bag and gave the women corn, pemmican, and wild turnip, and she taught them how to make a hearth fire to cook the food. White Buffalo Woman spoke to the children as well, and she told them they were the future, and that they would pray with the sacred pipe one day.

Then she spoke once more to all of the people. She told the Lakota that they were the purest among the tribes, and for that reason the holy pipe had been bestowed upon them. They had been chosen to take care of it for all Indian peoples.

The White Buffalo Woman then took leave, saying, "I shall see you again," and promising to return in times of need. She walked in the direction of the setting sun, and then she stopped and rolled over four times. The first time, she became a black buffalo, the second time a brown buffalo, the third time a red one, and the fourth time she rolled over, she turned into a white female buffalo calf.

Then the White Buffalo Woman disappeared over the horizon. After she was gone, great herds of buffalo appeared to give their own lives so that the people might survive. From that day on, the buffalo furnished their human relations with everything they needed, and the white buffalo became the most sacred living thing that a person could ever encounter.

This story is considered the most important of the many myths and legends handed down through generations of storytelling. Oral traditions were vital to Indian tribes. This was how they passed on their history to successive generations, how they instructed their young in the ways of the spirit, and how they paid homage to the sacred beings that inhabited their stories and myths.

The myth of the beautiful maiden who appears first in human form and then changes into a white buffalo calf was the reason why the Plains Indians so revered the white buffalo. Retelling the story strengthened and reaffirmed the power of the white buffalo. The power of the story still exists today.

△▰△▰△

Thundering across the Great Plains in great clouds of dust, vast herds of buffalo roamed the rich prairie lands that once stretched from Mexico to British Columbia, and from the foothills of the Rockies to the woodlands of the Midwest. Within such huge herds, estimated to be between 40 and 70 million animals, the number that were white is impossible to know. It can only be assumed that they were rare animals.

Whenever Indians saw a white buffalo, they killed it for sacrifice. The kill was usually taken back to camp for ceremony and ritual. Ethnographer George Dorsey studied the cults and societies of the Mandan and Hidatsa Indians in the late 1800s. Their rites included skinning the entire animal and tanning the hide with horns, nose, hooves, and tail intact. After removing the skin from the carcass, the hide was dried by the wind.

Among the Teton Sioux, the skinning knife and the arrow used to kill the buffalo were purified by smoking them over sweet grass. After the hide was tanned, it would be purified as well by medicine men. Only men of the tribe who had dreamed about or had had a vision of the white buffalo could eat the meat.

In 1882, anthropologist Alice Fletcher was allowed to view the White Buffalo Festival of the Hunkpapa, a division of the Teton Sioux. This highly important ceremony lasted several days and was held in great secrecy, with guards stationed outside of the medicine tipi. A virgin maiden, selected by the hunter who had killed the buffalo, was the only person allowed to touch the skin in the course of tanning it. After that, the hide could only be handled with sticks.

Because such strong power was associated with the white hides, Cheyenne women made captives tan them. Power could be dangerous as well as holy, and if for some reason the spirits became angry over the killing of the white buffalo, their fierceness would be directed toward the slaves, not toward the Cheyenne clanswomen. It was reported that the Mandans also used captives if possible.

The Blackfeet believed that the white buffalo belonged to the sun god and hung the white robe on a pole near the medicine man's tipi as an offering. Other tribes were also known to hang the white buffalo robe high on a pole, and it was common for the robe to stay there until it decomposed naturally in the wind and the weather.

For many tribes the white robe would become part of a sacred medicine bundle. A medicine bundle could be owned individually, or it might belong to a clan or to the whole tribe. It might contain animal skins, feathers, pigment, sweet grass, or sacred stones, depending on the vision of the person who had put the bundle together. With the proper ritual and reverence of those involved, the medicine bundle would be used to call upon supernatural powers to aid the Indians in war, during a hunt, in sickness, or at other times when magic was needed. In 1925, ethnographer Truman Michelson recorded an interview with a Fox war chief who claimed that, from one robe, five medicine bundles were made. The robe itself became part of the major bundle, and each hoof became part of four minor medicine bundles.

In another account, Michelson reported that the Fox honored the buffalo by performing the white buffalo dance. As recorded by ethnographers and anthropologists who studied Indian ways, the white buffalo was revered in many different Indian cultures. The Fox, for example, were not a Plains tribe; they lived farther east, at the edge of eastern woodlands near the Great Lakes. The Pueblo Indians of the desert Southwest also performed a buffalo dance. The buffalo was revered wherever its influence was felt.

There is documentation of at least one Cheyenne chief who wore a white robe into battle as protection from harm. The Mandans stored the white robe in its own rawhide case, taking it out only on special occasions, at which time the owner would be allowed to wear it. A painting by Swiss artist Karl Bodmer shows the women of the Mandans' White Buffalo Society (Color Plate 1), with one of the women wearing a full white robe and the others wearing headdresses of white hide. Bodmer, who traveled for two years with Alexander Phillip Maximilian, the prince of a small Prussian state, during his explorations of the West in the 1830s, produced about four hundred paintings of American Indians, depicting in detail their everyday and ceremonial lives.

The Mandans lived in permanent villages of earth lodges along the upper Missouri River, where they planted crops and hunted and traded for buffalo. Situated along the major water route to the West, they had extensive contact with whites, and their lives were well recorded in writings and artwork. Bodmer's painting shows the most honored elder women in the tribe dancing by the light of torches. As members of the White Buffalo Society, the women were responsible for holding ceremonies to attract bison each winter.

The legend of this particular ceremony begins with a man fasting during the coldest nights of winter. Each night he heard voices, and each night the voices came closer. On the fourth night, the voices were close enough that the man could hear what they were saying: "Put a child with them." Later, a man came by carrying two children, and he told the Mandan to return to the village and prepare a feast. He did what he was directed to do, and shortly thereafter a group of strange women entered the village. They performed a special dance, ate the feast foods, and left. These were buffalo women and the two children were buffalo children. Both of the children tried to escape but only one succeeded; the remaining one was raised as a Mandan.

The Mandans believed that when the women of the White Buffalo Society danced with the buffalo child in their midst, the buffalo would return to see the child. If the proper ritual and procession were followed faithfully, the ceremony would bring blizzards, driving the buffalo into the wooded river valleys where hunters could easily kill them. In this way, the Mandans never lacked for buffalo throughout the long, cold winters.

An almost identical headdress to the ones shown in Bodmer's painting is in the collection of the Museum of the American Indian in New York City. This headdress, collected in 1907 by ethnographer Gilbert Wilson, is Hidatsa rather than Mandan and is said to be the hide of an albino buffalo. When not in use, the headdresses were hung on the western or southern side of the tipis, the direction from which the buffalo came. The Bodmer painting gives some insight into the frequency of white buffalo. Although they were presumably rare, there were at least enough killed by the Mandans to make the required regalia for all of the women of the society. And the Mandans, it was reported, killed only white calves that were two years old or younger.

Another artist who achieved renown illustrating the Indians of the West was George Catlin. A portraitist from Philadelphia, he, too, documented the Mandan and other tribes during the 1830s. His journal writings included the following account of a white buffalo hide.

This beautiful and costly skin, when its history is known, will furnish a striking proof of the importance which they attach to these propitious offerings. But a few weeks since, a party of Mandans returned from the Mouth of the Yellow Stone, two hundred miles above, with information that a party of Blackfeet were visiting that place on business with the American Fur Company; and that they had with them a white buffalo robe for sale. This was looked upon as a subject of great importance by the chiefs, and one worthy of public consideration. A white buffalo robe is a great curiosity, even in the country of buffaloes, and will always command an almost incredible price, from its extreme scarcity, and then, from its being the most costly article of traffic in these regions, it is usually converted into a sacrifice, being offered to the Great Spirit, as the most acceptable gift that can be procured. Amongst the vast herds of buffaloes which graze on these boundless prairies, there is not one in a hundred thousand, perhaps, that is white; and when such a one is obtained, it is considered great medicine or mystery.

On the receipt of the intelligence above-mentioned, the chiefs convened in council, and deliberated on the expediency of procuring the white robe from the Blackfeet. . . . At the close of their deliberations, eight men were fitted out on eight of their best horses, who took from the Fur Company's store, on the credit of the chiefs, goods exceeding even the value of their eight horses; and they started for the Mouth of the Yellow Stone, where they arrived in due time, and made the purchase, by leaving the eight horses and all the goods which they carried; returning on foot to their own village, bringing home with them the white robe, which was looked upon by all eyes of the villagers as a thing that was vastly curious, and containing (as they expressed it) something of the Great Spirit. This wonderful anomaly laid several days in the chief's lodge, until public curiosity was gratified; and then it was taken by the doctors or high-priests, and with a great deal of form and mystery consecrated, and raised on the top of a long pole over the medicine-lodge; where it now stands in a group with the others, and will stand as an offering to the Great Spirit, until it decays and falls to the ground.

Catlin's account bespeaks the sacredness of the white robe. Disposing of the robe was also an important event. Allowing the hide to decay naturally was common in many tribes. The owner of a robe might be buried in it. Or the robe might be cut up into pieces to be given or traded away. Although the robes were valued for their sacredness, they were also highly valued in trade.

As early European explorers followed their native guides into Indian camps and villages for rest and food during their long journeys, they learned about the white buffalo and the prized white robe. In 1806, Alexander Henry wrote that the Hidatsa would part with a first-rate horse trained in war or buffalo hunting for a white hide. In 1851, Rudolph Friederich Kurz recorded that one white buffalo robe was traded for two good racehorses. Although there is no date for his source, Douglas E. Branch wrote that a white buffalo hide was worth ten to fifteen horses to the Mandans.

Most of the written history of the Indians comes from explorers and early ethnographers, as well as from the personal journals of frontiersmen and pioneers, and later from articles in prairie presses. The Indians did not have a written language. Their history was preserved in story and paint.

One of the most fascinating visual histories of the Plains Indians was the winter count robe. Winter count robes recorded the passing of the years. Tribal elders would decide upon the most memorable event of the year, and an image representing that event

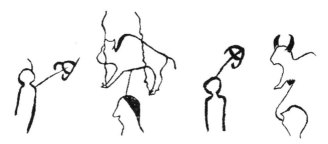

These drawings illustrate how events relating to white buffalo were recorded on winter count robes. The two with skulls indicate an individual "making medicine" with a white buffalo skin. The other two imply the possession of such a skin. (Drawings courtesy Nancy Jenkins/DMNH)

would be painted on a tanned buffalo hide. It was like a calendar in which the only notation for the year was made once each winter. It might chronicle a cosmic event, an important death, or contact with white men—whatever the elders considered most significant. The quality of the illustrations varied from artist to artist, though most of the drawings were simple in style, lacking the exacting detail of color and design found in Plains Indian quill- and beadwork. This was a form of record keeping.

One of the most impressive winter count robes was kept by Big Missouri, a member of the Sioux tribe. This extraordinary time line began in the winter of 1795–1796 and continued until 1926—a span of 131 years. The anthropology collection of the Denver Museum of Natural History has a muslin reproduction of the original hide. Kills Two, the Sioux medicine man who added the last illustration to the robe, interpreted the simple yet often enigmatic drawings, providing the following accounts of the five times when white buffalo appear.

1830   Indians believed the rare white buffalo sacred and the white hides were sacred possessions. Pompadour secured one and consecrated it in the name of his deceased son. Where such a hide was kept, the home was said to have good will for all men.

1831   Four white buffalo were killed. Largest number in history. Swift Bear owned the only horse fast enough to capture one.

Big Missouri's extraordinary winter count robe recorded the years between 1795–1796 and 1926 for one Lakota band. In that time, white buffalo were figured in the count five times. (John Anderson Collection, © Nebraska State Historical Society)

1848   Indian, Yellow Spider, custodian of sacred white buffalo hide.

1858   Sacred white buffalo cow killed by Swift Bear's band. They had the fleetest horses among the Sioux.

1873   Standing Cloud made keeper of the sacred white buffalo robe and master of ceremonies accompanying it.

The white buffalo was revered by the Plains tribes because it represented all buffalo, the very basis of the Indians' existence. Buffalo provided their human brothers with nearly everything they needed to survive. Rawhide, strong and durable, was used to make shields, trunks, parfleches (envelope-like cases for packing belongings), moccasin soles, knife sheaths, snowshoes, bridles, stirrups, saddles, and saddlebags. Tanned hides with the hair removed were sewn together to make tipi covers, summer clothing, and pouches. Hides with the hair left on became buffalo robes and blankets.

The meat was dried in the sun to make a kind of jerky, preserved in fat, or pounded into a meal and mixed with berries to make pemmican. Because it would not keep, the liver was eaten raw immediately after the kill; the intestines were made into sausage. Buffalo tongue was considered a delicacy. The brain was used in a tanning process; the women rubbed it into skins to create a soft, supple leather. Even the sinews could be used for lacings and bindings.

This spectacular Plains headdress incorporates the feathers of magpies, owls, and hawks, as well as the horns of a bison and Western trade goods (cloth and mirrors). As a whole it signifies both power and importance for the wearer. (DMNH AC.3621, © DMNH/Rick Wicker)

The Indians made soap from the fat; they fashioned bones into all manner of useful objects, from hoes to beads; they stretched sinew into thread and wove hair into rope; they used horns for spoons, cups, and ladles; they cooked and carried water in stomach paunches; they swatted flies away with buffalo tails; and they burned the dung for fuel.

Indian children played lacrosse with rawhide hoops and slid down snowy hills on sleds with runners made of rib bones. Buffalo horns, decorated with quills, beads, and feathers, became ceremonial headdresses. The skull became the altar around which dancers circled, shaking rattles made of rawhide and hooves.

From the time a child was born and carried in a buffalo hide cradle, to the time a body was laid to rest in a buffalo skin shroud, the Plains Indians were dependent on the great buffalo herds. It is not surprising that the buffalo was so revered.

It is unknown just how long Indians have lived on the plains, or in the rest of the Americas for that matter. The origin story of some tribes does include migrations, but for many other tribes the people emerged from the earth or were created from the land where they lived. A number of tribal spokespeople today are adamant about this point and are offended by a Western scientific interpretation. Indian fundamentalism doesn't include evolution any more than Christian fundamentalism does.

Archaeology tells a different story. For many decades the predominant hypothesis has been that people crossed the Bering Strait land bridge at the end of the Ice Age. Much of the world's water was contained in the glaciers that covered the northern region of the earth, leaving dry land between Siberia and the Americas. It was theorized that the ancestors of American Indians migrated across this land bridge, most likely following game. Archaeologists call these peoples "Paleo-Indians," and many sites in North America, including bison kills from the Great Plains, show evidence of being 9,500 to 11,000 years old.

A curious thing about science, though, is that new data and new techniques often change the old truths, and archaeology is no exception. Over the last decade or so, some exciting new archaeological sites have been found in South America that date to more than twenty thousand years ago, based on radiocarbon analysis. The new information has not been readily accepted by the archaeological community, and the scientists who discovered these sites continue their critical study of the area to determine whether they are as old as the initial tests indicate. If so, these sites will revolutionize American archaeology and the interpretation of when and how various peoples came to the Americas.

Regardless of migration patterns or origin stories, wherever people settled, they adapted to their particular environment. Archaeologists have excavated artifacts of these early people, and many of the items reveal a connection to the natural world. Delicately carved stone pipes with images of ravens, raccoons, ducks, and other woodland animals have been recovered from ancient burial mounds in Ohio, Indiana, and Illinois, as well as ceramic bowls decorated with pictures of the roseate spoonbill, a bird long extinct in the Midwest. The tribes of the Pacific Northwest left behind totems and stone carvings of whales, fishes, and sea mammals. Desert tribes revered the coyote, the bighorn sheep, and the snake—images of which they etched onto canyon walls. For the Indians of the Great Plains the buffalo defined the universe.

Early Plains Indians stayed mostly on the periphery of the vast, semiarid grasslands. During the cold and harsh months, they camped in the shelter of wooded river bottoms. Winters were lean times, and the Indians were lucky if a herd of buffalo wandered close to camp. More likely they would find stragglers, and with loud shouts and arms waving, the hunters would scare the animals into snowdrifts, trapping them there for the kill. Buffalo harvested in winter were valued for their thick coats of fur, which made the best robes; autumn kills provided the best meat, after the animals had fattened up over the summer.

During the summer months, the nomadic tribes ventured farther into the interior of the Great Plains, following the herds on their yearly migrations. For hunting purposes, the tribes split into smaller bands, perhaps twenty to thirty people in a family group, often related by blood. Disguised in wolf or coyote skins, the hunters would creep up on hands and knees to stalk the buffalo, which might stand more than six feet tall at the hump and weigh more than a ton. Once they were within close range, the hunters used spears or bows and arrows to kill their prey. It was a dangerous method of hunting.

There were safer and more efficient ways. One of these was the buffalo "jump." Waving robes in the air, shouting, and making a commotion, the Indians would cause the herd to stampede to the edge of a steep cliff, sending the animals plunging over the side to be killed by the fall. Large numbers of animals were harvested in this way, and the Indians often killed more than they could use.

Another ambush technique was the "surround," which was a sturdy corral built at the bottom of a

As early as 9,500 years ago, ancient North Americans hunted bison by driving them over cliffs. If they were not killed in the fall, surviving bison were dispatched with spears. (Courtesy Thomas F. Kehoe)

sloping cliff. In summer, the slope might be covered with dung mixed with water to make it slippery; in winter, water would be poured on the slope to form an ice sheet. Shouting and waving, the Indians drove the buffalo down the slope. Even if the animals in front tried to stop, they would be pushed down the slippery incline by the ones behind them. The animals trapped in the corral were killed by hunters waiting at the bottom.

Herding animals into corrals for the kill has roots in ancient hunting practices. One of the many incredible cave paintings discovered in Lascaux, France, depicts a skillfully drawn corral with a series of black dots that form a lane leading into it. At the Spanish site of Bojadillas, there are also numerous

Rather than using jumps, some tribes stampeded bison into surrounds, or corrals made of logs. This technique was used not only in North America but also in Europe, 20,000–30,000 years ago. (Courtesy Amon Carter Museum, Fort Worth, Texas)

Stone Age hunting scenes, including one of a corral with a doe inside. Outside the corral are figures of men with bows. Is the doe bait, and are the men waiting for their quarry?

The animals drawn by the ancients were probably sources of food, such as bison, horses, musk ox, and mammoths, as well as dangerous adversaries, such as cave lions and the woolly rhinoceros. Bison are among the most commonly pictured animals in the prehistoric caves of Europe. These paintings offer revealing insights into the lives of Paleolithic peoples. Especially intriguing are the half-bison/half-human figures.

The walls of the Chauvet Cave in the Ardeche region of southern France show an image of a bison head with human legs, most likely a man wearing a buffalo cape. Based on radiocarbon dating, the paintings in this cave are approximately thirty thousand years old. A similar painting, even more clearly a man wearing a bison hide, complete with the animal's hump and the tail trailing behind, can be seen in the

This bison-man figure is depicted on the walls of the Cave of the Three Brothers in France. It is much more recent than the one discovered in Chauvet Cave, being only thirteen thousand years old. (Drawing courtesy Nancy Jenkins/DMNH)

Gabillou Cave, also in southern France. We can only speculate as to the meanings of these images. Are they young men being initiated as hunters? Are they hunters reliving a successful hunt? Or are these half-bison/half-human figures shamans invoking hunting magic?

In virtually all cultures that have depended on hunting, people have tried to influence the hunt through ritual. In Plains Indian cultures, "buffalo callers" performed ceremonies to attract the animals to the buffalo jumps and surrounds. These shamans had special knowledge of how to bring buffalo to the people, especially in times of hunger. The caller might dress in an animal skin, though not necessarily a buffalo hide, and dance back and forth until the herd began to follow him as he moved toward the

The buffalo caller was a shaman who had special powers to bring the bison into the buffalo jump or surround so that his people would not starve. (Courtesy Thomas F. Kehoe)

jump or the surround. Other members of the tribe—
men, women, and children—would fall in behind the
herd, driving the buffalo faster and faster toward the
jump. The caller would leap out of the animals' way at
the last minute, and the buffalo would tumble over
the cliff or slide down the slope into the surround.

A caller might have used a buffalo stone in his ritual. The stone would be carried in the shaman's
medicine bundle along with other sacred objects
used to invoke hunting magic. Unwrapping the bundle, the caller would sing and pray over the objects,
calling for the return of the buffalo. The Blackfeet
called these stones *iniskim*, and they favored ammon-
ites that they found on the plains. The Indians
thought that these fossilized seashells looked like
sleeping buffalo. According to Blackfoot legend, the
first buffalo stone revealed itself to a young woman
who was out gathering firewood during a time of
famine. The stone told her of a ritual that would call
the buffalo to her. She and her husband performed
the ritual as they had been instructed and the buffalo came. From that time on, people performed the
same ritual whenever they needed to attract buffalo.

Archaeologists have examined buffalo kill sites
throughout the plains. At the Jones-Miller site near
Wray, Colorado, a team led by Dr. Dennis Stanford
of the Smithsonian Institution recovered more than
forty thousand bison bones. They estimated that the
bones represented at least 250 buffalo and that they
were probably about ten thousand years old. The
bones were found in a corral-type impoundment
along with stone points and butchering tools.

The Jones-Miller bison kill site is located near Wray, Colorado. This site yielded more than forty thousand bones and artifacts that helped archaeologist Dennis Stanford reconstruct the activities associated with the kill. (Courtesy Dennis Stanford/Smithsonian Institution)

Little evidence of ceremonial artifacts at the kill sites has been excavated to date. Within this particular impoundment, however, the archaeologists found a deep posthole. Because it was located in the middle of the enclosure, it evidently wasn't part of the fence that contained the buffalo. Next to the posthole was a miniature Hell's Gap point, what appeared to be a bone flute, and the butchered remains of a dog. Could this have been where the shaman performed his ritual to call the buffalo to the surround? Did he play the flute and sacrifice the dog as part of the hunting magic? Did the miniature arrowhead symbolize the kill to take place? Did the posthole hold a flag aloft, showing the people where to drive the buffalo? These are intriguing questions; the answers may never be known.

Plains Indians adopted new methods of hunting as they absorbed influences from other cultures. Before the introduction of the horse, they had hunted and traveled on foot, using domesticated dogs as pack animals. When Coronado and other Spanish explorers entered the Southwest in the mid-1500s, they rode on horseback. Through raiding and trading, Indians obtained the horse as well, and within the course of two hundred years, tribes throughout the plains had adopted this method of travel. The horse brought revolutionary changes to the Plains culture.

Horses were specially trained for hunting buffalo, as agility and speed were needed to avoid being gored during the hunt. A buffalo horse was a prized possession. If it was suspected that a horse raiding party from another tribe was nearby, a hunter would bring his buffalo horse into the tipi for the night, forcing family members to sleep outside. The horse became a standard of wealth and prestige. A wealthy man not only had many horses, he might also have many wives, for the more successful he was at hunting, the more wives he needed to tan the buffalo hides.

On horseback the Plains Indians could travel farther and faster. A domesticated dog trailing a travois was very limited in how much weight it could transport. With horses, Indians could carry more belongings, such as larger tipis, and they could haul more meat and hides from buffalo kill sites. They had more mobility and ventured far onto the open plains to follow the migrating herds, and they traveled greater distances to trade with other tribes. With the horse, the Indian culture of the Great Plains flourished, reaching its zenith in the mid-1800s.

Another influence was the gun, and again Indians adapted to it quickly. Explorers, frontiersmen, and traders from the east brought the rifle to the plains, exchanging guns for buffalo hides at the trading posts that sprang up along the major westward routes. With the gun, the Indian became even more efficient at hunting buffalo, swooping in close to the herd and quickly killing off animals along the outer edges. Indians continued to use buffalo jumps and surrounds for slaughtering large numbers of buffalo, for the robes were a measure of exchange for the white man's goods. One buffalo robe could be bartered for a gallon kettle or a yard and a half of calico. Four buffalo robes would buy a Hudson Bay blanket, and eight buffalo robes could be traded for an ordinary riding horse or one gun with a hundred rounds of ammunition. The Indians no longer hunted only for sustenance; they now hunted for commerce as well.

The Plains Indians were very observant and highly adaptive, but there was one thing to which they could not adapt: the foreign civilization encroaching on their lands. Following the explorers, trappers, and traders came the multitudes: wagon trains of pioneers heading west to settle the frontier; forty-niners looking to strike it rich in the goldfields of California; the railroad pushing across the plains, building towns along the rights-of-way granted them by a government looking to people a continent. With the Homestead Act of 1862, free land became available to anyone who could work it.

"Our nation is melting away like the snow on the sides of the hills where the sun is warm, while your people are like the blades of grass in spring when the summer is coming," Red Cloud, the great Sioux chief, told government officials in 1870. As the traditional hunting grounds of the Plains Indians were shrinking, so too were the herds.

A number of factors led to the decimation of the buffalo. The Indians themselves were hunting more animals for trade. Buffalo runners, hired by the railroad to procure food for the crews laying track across the prairie, became highly proficient at downing large numbers of animals quickly. William Cody, better known as Buffalo Bill, boasted that he had killed forty-eight buffalo in less than an hour. Professional hide hunters killed off massive numbers, often just skinning the animals and leaving the meat to rot on the prairie. Policy makers in Washington decided that the best way to eliminate "the Indian problem" was to eliminate their source of food, and the government encouraged the slaughter of the remaining buffalo herds. By the end of the nineteenth century, fewer than a thousand buffalo were left, a staggering reduction from the estimated 40 to 70 million that had once roamed the Great Plains.

With the Indians subdued, the government started moving them onto reservations. But the conflicts between whites and Indians continued: Treaties were made and treaties were broken; Indian wars erupted on the plains. It was a clash of economies as well as a clash of ideologies. Indians believed the land was the sacred giver of life and that it belonged to all, that no one person could own it. The white man had a different perspective. He looked upon the vast open spaces as so much real estate to be bought and sold and saw the land as the raw material for building an expanding nation.

By the late 1880s, the buffalo were gone and the Indians' way of life had vanished. Required to live on reservations to qualify for rations, the Indians' only other choice was to leave and face starvation. They were dependent on the government for food and housing. The brave warriors and mounted hunters that had ruled the Great Plains were now on welfare, their spirits broken.

In the midst of this bleak scenario, a ray of hope shone through. A prophet appeared. A young Paiute

Indian from Nevada promised the return of old ways in which there would be no white men, the great buffalo herds would return to the plains, and all Indians—living and dead—would exist together peacefully. All the Indians had to do was pray and dance in the slow, sedate style the new messiah had seen in his vision.

The ceremony became known as the "Ghost Dance" because it was said that the dead would come back to life. This religious movement quickly gained momentum as it spread from reservation to reservation throughout the plains, uniting many different tribes. Fearful of uprisings, the U.S. government outlawed the Ghost Dance. Its adherents continued the practice in secret, in remote corners of reservations away from the eyes of the Indian agents who watched over them. Efforts to stop the movement failed, until it ended in tragedy at Wounded Knee, where more than 150 Sioux men, women, and children were massacred on the South Dakota plains. The year was 1890.

In the decades that followed, many traditional Indian ways were lost through assimilation as the government attempted to force Indians to conform to white society. Indian schoolchildren were not allowed to speak their native tongue in reservation schools. The government tried to eradicate native religion and prohibited traditional ceremonies. The Sun Dance, the most holy of Plains Indian rituals, was declared illegal in many states. Elders tried to keep the old ways alive, but often the younger generations were not interested, choosing instead to become modern Americans and leave their people's traditions behind.

Many Indians converted to Christianity, taught by missionaries in reservation churches and schools. But often what evolved were hybrid religious concepts, blending the Native American belief that all things are sacred with the acceptance of Christian tenets. Indian spirituality had always embraced the old and the new in a continually evolving view of the world. Even traditional stories were open to new interpretations.

The story of the White Buffalo Woman ends with the maiden turning into a buffalo and then changing color four times, from black to brown to red, and finally to white. A hundred years ago, these colors might have been said to symbolize the four directions or the four seasons of the year. Today there are elders who interpret this aspect of the story as representing the four colors of humankind. This modern interpretation is not surprising in an age when peoples all over the world are linked via global economies and technologies.

The story of the White Buffalo Woman did not die out. So important was this myth that it endured while other Indian legends did not. Does the birth of a female white calf signify a return to the power of the buffalo? A century after the Plains Indians were crushed by a more forceful civilization, Indian nations are now regaining their rights and are growing in political and economic power. This resurgence is evident in many arenas.

Within the legal system, there has been an impressive string of successes as tribes throughout North America have won court cases to reinstate—or be compensated for—tribal lands taken when treaties were broken. Indians have regained access to their sacred lands, as well as to fishing and hunting rights. With the passage of the Native American Graves Protection and Repatriation Act, native peoples are reclaiming holy objects as well as human remains that were taken without their consent.

New economic development can also be seen on many reservations. The introduction of casino gambling, for better or worse, has pumped incredible amounts of money into tribal coffers. Establishing tribal bison herds is another step toward economic self-sufficiency, a move aided by the Inter-Tribal Bison Cooperative. Native American corporations are now major players in determining how the natural resources within their lands are to be used, and they are increasingly setting the terms for fair remuneration for access to these natural resources. With new legal power and the financial resources to back it up, many tribes across the country are moving into a new era of prosperity.

Even among tribes still caught in a web of poverty (unemployment on the Pine Ridge Reservation in South Dakota hovers around a staggering 75 percent), there is renewed interest in traditional ways. High school and elementary school students can now study the Lakota language, and elective courses offer classes in Sioux history and culture. Youngsters join clubs to learn traditional music and dances, and they participate with pride in tribal powwows.

Is the birth of the white buffalo the symbol or the cause of this resurgence? Or is it just a coincidence? To a large extent, it depends on whom you ask. But there is more to be considered here. Just as the buffalo in the story of the White Buffalo Woman changed color four times, so too has Miracle, the white calf born on the Heiders' farm. Coincidence? Or prophecy?

A century ago, the Ghost Dance united Indian tribes in the hope of a better future; today, Miracle seems to have inspired a similar sentiment, but now on a global scale. People from around the world have traveled to Janesville, Wisconsin, to see the buffalo calf—Indians and non-Indians alike. The story of the White Buffalo Woman prophesied that she would return in times of need. Does this refer to the needs of Indian people—or of all people? Floyd Hand, the Lakota elder who predicted the birth of Miracle and the death of her sire, claims that Miracle was born to non-Indians to show that her message was meant for all people, not just Native Americans. The prophecy has indeed taken on global implications, for Miracle has captured the attention of the world.

Native American beliefs have evolved with the passage of time, but the main tenet that has always held true, that is the very basis for all Indian religions, is the knowledge that the earth and all that belongs to the earth are sacred and should be revered. As the world stands at the end of the Industrial Revolution, the planet soiled and polluted from 150 years of industrial production, people around the world recognize the need to protect the earth. Environmental awareness is not limited to the industrialized nations; all nations see the health of the earth as essential to the future. Today there is a growing consciousness of the need for a worldview that honors the earth—just as the American Indians always have.

Poised at the edge of the Information Age—the next frontier in human history—are we also seeing a return to the old ways? Has the Indian prophecy handed down through generations now come true? Has the White Buffalo Woman returned to the people in a time of need? These are very serious responsibilities to rest on the shoulders of one small buffalo calf named Miracle.

CHAPTER THREE

WHAT DO THE ELDERS SEE?

Many people, myself included, go into anthropology because we are obsessed with the question "why?" This is particularly true when the question pertains to how societies work and what motivates people. The sacred aspects of life are some of the most fascinating—yet also some of the most sensitive and potentially easily misunderstood—subjects that two people from different cultures can discuss. But that is what anthropologists do.

Although I am not a social anthropologist and the study of religion and spirituality is not one of my specialties, I have been very fortunate to have known and talked to some truly extraordinary spiritual leaders. While living in Thailand, I sat and drank tea as I learned something of Buddhism from young monks and a very energetic abbot. Another time, in Indianapolis of all places, I sat in a living room with a small group of people viewing slides of Tibet. Only later in the evening did I find out that the gentleman sitting next to me was the brother of the Dalai Lama.

Directing an archaeological project on the island of Yap in Micronesia gave me the opportunity to interview village chiefs as well as a man who was the last in a long line of canoe magicians. I have also discussed Catholic views on evolution with monastic Benedictine brothers. And, with the birth of the white buffalo, I have talked at length with Indian elders. Having grown up in small-town, midwestern Methodism, the study of anthropology and these exotic encounters have shown me a diversity of spirituality that I otherwise could not have imagined.

Scholar Joseph Campbell once said that American Indians may be the most spiritual people on earth. In their world, all things are sacred. In the world of the Plains Indian, the white buffalo is especially sacred. Stories from many different tribes speak of the buffalo as a nation not unlike the human nation. The bison have human attributes: They talk, hold council, advise, and help their human brothers. The story of White Buffalo Woman is only one of many stories about the buffalo nation. Although the particular story recounted in this book is Lakota, many Plains peoples share similar stories, if not the exact details. Farther from the plains, this story is less likely to hold such power. Just as the story's impact has changed across the landscape, so too has the legend of White Buffalo Woman changed through time. Yet the story still lives today, and through recent events it is gaining the attention of a new generation of Indians and non-Indians.

To the Lakota the birth of the white buffalo calf was a momentous occasion—an event foretold in prophecy. Other tribes, depending on how important the myth of the White Buffalo Woman has been to their culture, viewed the event differently. For some tribes and elders, the calf was simply a curiosity, something to wonder about. For others, Miracle's arrival was no more important than any other item on the evening news. I spoke with Pueblo Indians, for example, to whom the event held little or no significance.

I have purposely chosen not to compare nineteenth-century versions of the White Buffalo Woman story with the one retold in this book. My intent is not to judge for historical accuracy. In fact, some aspects of the story are clearly different from versions recorded a hundred years ago. To me this serves to reinforce the idea of a living religion attempting to interpret the contemporary world.

In these days of resurgent Indian identity, Indian peoples no longer are willing to allow non-Indians to interpret their spirituality. For that reason I asked elders from three different tribes to tell me what they thought about Miracle and her spiritual significance. I conducted interviews with each of the elders, sent them copies of the transcript of our talk, and asked them to make corrections where necessary. The rest of this chapter presents our conversations in the question-and-answer format in which they were conducted. I have edited some redundant statements for the sake of length. However, the answers to the questions are the words of the speakers.

ARVAL LOOKING HORSE

A Lakota spiritual leader and teacher, Arval Looking Horse is the Keeper of the Sacred Pipe. The sacred white buffalo calf pipe has been handed down through nineteen generations of the Looking Horse family, since it was first given to the Lakota Sioux by the White Buffalo Woman. His grandmother was Keeper of the Sacred Pipe before him. Prior to her death, she had a vision that told her to pass the pipe on to her grandson. Arval was just twelve years old when he was given this sacred honor. If a generation is considered to be 20 years, the pipe has been in his family for at least 380 years.

Arval Looking Horse was born and raised on the Cheyenne River Reservation in South Dakota, where he lives today with his wife and daughter. He has traveled the world over representing the Lakota people, participating in world peace ceremonies and Native American prayer services. As Keeper of the Sacred Pipe, he is responsible for keeping the sacred pipe ceremonies alive and passing on the knowledge of them to future generations.

You are the carrier of the sacred white buffalo calf pipe. What does that mean?

This is the pipe given by Buffalo Calf Woman to Tanka Wasla Najin, my ancestor. The pipe stays in the bloodline. When the keeper is going to the spirit world, he or she would have a dream as to whom to pass it on to. A woman can also be the keeper.

As I understand it, the prophecy associated with the white buffalo says that she will return to the people in times of need. Is that correct?

When she returns, it is a validation of the prayers our people have made. We pray to complete ourselves spiritually, to feel good about ourselves and the future.

Over the last hundred years, lots of people have lost their way of life. During that time, we did not have freedom of religion. Many of the stories were not handed down. But now we're getting the old ways back. The white buffalo and the return of the buffalo are part of the return to old ways.

There are prayers for the seventh generation. The seventh generation from Wounded Knee was in 1990. In that year, we had a "wiping of tears" ceremony at Wounded Knee. We know that this seventh generation is a crossroads for us. The people prayed for their way of life. If we don't live in the right way, we will be lost. That is why the white buffalo calf has been born now. It is a sign that the prayers are being fulfilled. People are taking notice.

The signs are good; people are coming back to the religion. If we don't go back to our way of life, our ceremonies, when White Buffalo Woman appears, then that will be the end of our way of life.

When I was very young, they killed off the buffalo and put people on the reservation. Today, buffalo are coming back and the culture is coming back. Even bison ranchers, non-Indian ranchers, are seeing it in a spiritual way.

Lots of people are having dreams, they are more open, and the white buffalo appears in their dreams.

Do you think that the calf born in Wisconsin two years ago is important?

I grew up hearing about these prophecies, that a white buffalo would be born in hardship times. It would be a sign that our prayers were still being answered. The calf being born to the Heiders doesn't change its significance. The calf is still sacred.

Floyd Hand told me that the calf's being born at the Heiders' farm meant that the message of White Buffalo Woman is for all people, not just for the Lakota and not just for Indians. Is that why Miracle is important?

When we pray, we pray to walk in the sacred manner. It is a message for all people, not just Indians. We live on Turtle Island—a sacred island. The whole plains, the whole continent, is Turtle Island. It is sacred land. A long time ago, Turtle Island was occupied by very spiritual people. They knew their territories. Those ideas are coming back. The ideas of responsibility, leadership, and the importance of the environment are coming back.

The Heiders have gone about it in the right way. They are good people. They have tried to do the right things. They are good listeners.

Does it make any difference that its color has changed from white to black to red to blonde?

White Buffalo Woman came from the west. When she left, she went to the west. The first time she rolled over, she was black. The second time, she was red. The third time she rolled over, she was the color of buckskin. The fourth time, she was white. Through our prayers, we ask that Miracle will change back to white.

What do the changes in color symbolize?

Every medicine person or spiritual leader makes their own interpretations. Things that were written a hundred years ago may not be interpreted the same way today. It is a sign that the religion is alive and well.

If the colors were interpreted as sacred, or if they were interpreted just as being part of the story of White Buffalo Woman, that's all right. Today, if the elders think that the colors represent the four colors of mankind, then that's what they think. You can't question the elders.

As far as you are concerned, is there a difference between an albino calf, a white calf, and a buffalo-Charolais cross?

Yes. The calf has to be pure. If it's mixed with cattle, it is not pure.

Have you heard about the white buffalo recently born on the Pine Ridge Reservation?

Yes. The elders have accepted it as pure buffalo. It is one of the four white buffalo that were prophesied to be born alive and well.

Right now there appear to be three white buffalo and three partially white buffalo. Are they all sacred in the same way?

The ones that are born partially white are sacred too. They are different and they are significant to the ceremonies. These are signs that the prophecy is alive and well.

The elders have said that there would be four white calves born and they would live. Miracle was the first one born in 1994. This summer, a calf was born at Pine Ridge. The elders have accepted this one. Another calf, an albino one, also was born this summer in North Dakota. It is sacred. One more will be born.

Readings from the last century all say that when white buffalo were encountered, they were sacrificed. Should that be done today?

No, they should not be sacrificed. They bring people together. The white buffaloes carry the message to the people.

When you look at Miracle or one of the other white buffalo, what do you see?

I see the history of my family and the Lakota people when I look at the calf. My family has kept the sacred pipe for nineteen generations. I feel very comfortable and honored to see the white buffalo being born and to see them being honored by others.

The white buffalo is a sign. Many nations have these signs, and all of these signs validate our prayers and point toward world peace and harmony. On August 27, 1997, there will be a day of peace and harmony in New Orleans. The spirit of White Buffalo Woman is part of that.

JOHN AND VIRGENE TARNESSE

John Tarnesse is a Sun Dance Chief of the Eastern Shoshone tribe and a member of the Seed Eater Clan. He was born on the Wind River Reservation in Wyoming. For much of his early adult life, he went to school and hitchhiked around western North America. His wife, Virgene, comes from a line of medicine people, and she is also active in traditional Shoshone spirituality and ritual. Each of them is a reserved yet powerful personality. Talking with them together was an energizing experience.

Are you a member of any society for which the white buffalo has special meaning?

JOHN: I am not a member of any white buffalo society. I don't really think there was a white buffalo society among the Shoshone. But we have lost much of our culture. If there was one, we don't know about it now. When I was growing up, I saw many dances, particularly in winter and spring months. There were buffalo dances. The dancers were probably warriors.

Are you a member of any other societies?

VIRGENE: John is a Sun Dance Chief and a traditional dancer, as are those in his family line. [In the old days] they knew the buffalo dance, chokecherry dance, sun dance, war bonnet, tail feather, grass dance, wolf dances, owl dance, and other dances.

Do you remember when you first heard about the white buffalo?

JOHN: At Bull Lake on the Fort Washakie Reservation. When I was growing up, I heard the story that some of our people found some buffalo, among which was a white buffalo. They chased the buffalo toward a drop. They were running the buffalo toward the edge of the mountain. One buffalo didn't fall. He ran down the side of the mountain and down into the lake. It was a white buffalo bull. When I was growing up, you could hear the grunts and bellows of the bull in the winter.

Are there any ceremonies or dances associated with the white buffalo?

JOHN: At that particular ground there was a dance from midnight to midmorning called "blanket dance." Those dances had a lot of the meaning. Now, no one knows.

Do the Shoshone people have the legend of White Buffalo Woman?

JOHN: We probably had a similar legend, but many now believe the books and stories that have come from the Sioux tribes. The story of the White Buffalo Woman is a legend of spirituality, and it opens the teaching of the spiritual world. The white buffalo is a spirit that can change from a bird to a woman to a buffalo. It appeared to the Lakota as a woman but appeared to other tribes as other things. The same spirit appears to different people in different ways.

VIRGENE: The ceremony became the spiritual reality—it is medicine. It is different from the physical side of life. The white buffalo calf in Wisconsin [Miracle] doesn't mean anything to us. Our ceremonies are the spiritual part.

Are there any other stories or legends about the white buffalo that you know?

JOHN: The white buffalo is very strong in its spiritual powers. One had to be very wise and very courageous to show his people how to bring strength to life. That person could kill a white buffalo and would keep the hide. The hide would be used to make a medicine bundle. He who had the white buffalo hide was the spiritual leader. I have never seen a white buffalo medicine bundle.

Who could prepare the hide?

JOHN: It didn't matter who prepared the hide; all people had respect for all living things. However, the one who killed the white buffalo usually prepared the hide.

Who could eat the flesh?

JOHN: The meat was eaten by the warriors, with offerings and prayers of thanks. The one who killed the white buffalo would dry the flesh and bring it out at ceremonial times.

They would give the spirits some of the flesh and sing songs that everything would come back again; that our lakes would be filled up again, that the rivers would be full, and that the flatlands would be replenished, both the spiritual side and the human side.

They would ask that the old ones and the young ones would learn as they go on into the spiritual world. They would pray, "Now our old ones have gone into the spiritual world; it is time to put our feet into the moccasins of our old people and begin teaching our young ones. So that they learn our sacred ways."

What would happen to the hide?

JOHN: The hide became part of the medicine bundle. At ceremonial times, the one who had killed the buffalo wore this bundle, showing that he was the spiritual leader with many powers. He could heal. That was his purpose.

He who made the medicine bundle did other ceremonies in his healing. He taught young mankind, like teachers today. He taught the young ones about going through the form of becoming a warrior, and about the concerns of the people. They would go to him for those matters.

What would happen to the skull?

JOHN: He who killed the white buffalo would offer the skull to the spirits at any of the four sacred points. The four spiritualities are sexuality, temper, craziness, and humor. Humor overrides the other three spiritualities.

He would take the skull with the flesh still on it to the sacred area and place the skull there as an offering. He would leave it out there for up to a year. Then he would return and pick up the skull. By then, it possessed spiritual prowess, and this is where the leadership of certain ceremonies—such as the sun dance—began. We are starving for wisdom, and this is why the skull is in the sun dance. It will help bring back the buffalo to teach us.

As always, the buffalo would return from the travels of its time from Canada to far south. They were holistic in their migrations. They made everything become greener where they passed. When they walked the earth, it was like they plowed the earth and then fertilized it. That's how the skull was used. It all turned back. It brings the earth back to life. It brings our culture back to life.

Do you know of any winter count robes or other Shoshone images of white buffalo?

JOHN: There are not many traditionalists left who know the images or what they mean. I don't know of any images, except in a frog form, around Bull Lake—about eight miles away. It is the white buffalo that went into Bull Lake.

Is there any prophecy associated with the white buffalo?

VIRGENE: The white buffalo is related to the directions and the sacred blanket. In my family, who are medicine people, there is a form of prophecy that will come about. It pertains to the coming of the Indian messiah—not Jesus Christ, but another messiah.

To us, the white buffalo means death. The backside of death is the sacred side and the holy side of life. It is prophesied that the red man messiah would bring life back to the dead through the songs he sings and the way he lays out his feathers on the buffalo robe. In the way he lays down the feathers and does his ceremony, he brings back life into the world, into the rocks and everything. Old man of the north direction is death.

When John conducts the sun dance—I have seen it—the white buffalo enters the dance area. We have seen the white buffalo spirit knock a man down who then has a vision. The white buffalo is the sacred side that comes into the sun dance. The sun dance represents the sacred and holy side of life.

When a man is knocked down, he goes into the spiritual realm and the spirit gives him guidance. He can't take too much at one time. But his awakening is there, like coming out of a dead sleep. He's healed— mind, body, and soul. That's the beginning of his spiritual awakening.

The understanding of the white buffalo is that it comes every year and covers the land, and that is death. It is like God weeding his garden. He takes out the old people and the sick. Laying the white robe is the snow that covers the earth. The sacred blanket slowly disappears and brings back life. That's why these ceremonies are in the winter and not the summer.

Do the Shoshone people think that the calf born in Wisconsin two years ago is important? Do you think it is important?

JOHN: Yes, it is important. We as humans have to see something. Being born white, the spiritual world sent it. The old medicine has gone on, passed on. This one is in our generation. It means that the White Buffalo Woman exists.

These humans that give offerings are desecrating themselves. The spirit has been given; it's already here. It is important to all tribes, to all red nations.

Miracle's half sister was born with white legs. She is important, she is very strong, she too is telling us that things are coming back.

Does it make any difference that Miracle's color has changed from white to black to red to blonde?

JOHN: Yes. They knew that it would change color. It means that all colors of people are going to go back to their cultures because of the changes taking place in the white buffalo calf. All nations should go back to the reality of their own cultures. This calf is important for everyone, not just Indian people.

VIRGENE: The four colors in the sun dance lodge are like four segments of a pie. They are the four quarters, the four stages of life, and the four races of human beings. John's aunt and uncle danced over the four colors within the lodge, and it represents going from beginning to end through four seasons, and the cycle from young to old, and the return of the four colors of mankind back to their cultures and their religions. When the white buffalo changed its colors, it symbolized these changes.

FLOYD HAND

An elder of the Oglala Sioux, Floyd Hand grew up on the Pine Ridge Reservation in South Dakota. His Indian name is Looks For Buffalo. Floyd Hand had a premonition of the birth of the white buffalo on the day that Miracle was born. He also had a vision that Miracle's sire would die, and he traveled to Janesville, Wisconsin, to tell the Heiders. A few days later, the sire did indeed die.

I had read some newspaper articles that had quoted Floyd Hand, and I knew that he had an extraordinary perspective on religion and spirituality. A Native American who has also embraced Catholicism and the Episcopalian faith, he sees connections between religious traditions that others would not. In some ways, his view of the world is very Lakota, and at the same time, it transcends cultural boundaries. My interview with Floyd Hand was a remarkable discussion of spirituality and the meaning of the white buffalo.

I know that the white buffalo and all buffalo are important to the Lakota. Are you a member of any society for which the white buffalo is particularly important?

No, but all the Lakota have a responsibility. My grandfather killed a white buffalo in the early 1800s. His name was Kills White Buffalo. White Buffalo Woman came to the Sioux nation, and we have a responsibility for teaching and passing on the seven rituals. The Oglala don't want modernization. The Oglala maintain the traditions.

When did you first know that the white buffalo calf was going to be born?

I knew on the day it was born—I am a medicine man.

Did you know where it was going to be born?

No, I didn't know where she was going to be born.

Do you remember when you first heard about the white buffalo?

I didn't hear about it; I was taught. The white buffalo is the image of the blessed Virgin Mary. In 1968, she first showed her image on the wall at my grandmother's house. I told my high school teacher at Red Cloud School about it. He was a priest and he told me that no Indian people ever see these holy people.

In 1988, twenty years later, I lived in Minneapolis. The same image appeared on my bedroom wall. This time, I could make out clearly that she had on a chiffon dress with rainbow colors. She had a beautiful face and dark, piercing eyes. In Indian language—Lakota—she said, "Tell them I am coming." She said it three times.

What was her message?

Her first message was that all four nations have

violated their responsibilities. "Therefore, I have returned to give you the message from God, just as old legend says. The power of the woman has returned and will lead the nations. It will begin from the east in the yellow nation."

The second message was that evil will destroy evil. A great famine will occur between 1997 and 1999. There will be many deserts on this earth. The government will be in turmoil. People in power will lose their positions and a new government will be formed.

The third message was that there will be destruction through nature and manmade disasters. There will occur fires, floods, hurricanes, tornadoes, tidal waves, earthquakes, and wars. Cities will be especially hard hit with gas and electrical disasters. Her prediction is that in the twenty-first century, there will be a whole cloud that covers the earth for 120 to 140 days. And then on the twenty-first day of the twenty-first year of the twenty-first century, peace, love, and harmony will return through the guidance of the woman.

The fourth message was that new nations will restore the beginning of the new world from the old world. This prediction coincides with the revelations in the Bible.

She will change herself to many nations, beginning as white, then red, then black, then yellow. Eventually she will go to gray. This is the basis for the prediction that Miracle would change colors. In fact, she has. Her colors have changed from white to black to yellow and now red.

How were you chosen to be part of the prophecy?
Back in 1954, my uncle, Frank Afraid of Horses, and I were sitting next to his cabin. He pointed at the full moon and wanted me to remember that the whole world would be corrupted by losing its spirituality, and that in my lifetime, I would witness something that no man had ever seen before.

My uncle said I must go out and learn about his relatives, meaning the yellows, blacks, and whites. In Frank Afraid of Horses' teachings, there are three male leaders that have dominated those nations. Each of these leaders, and all men, have a hard time showing compassion for the things he is responsible for. This buffalo calf lady will return, and she is going to teach us to remember what God has given us. I was to prepare myself for this time.

I also was told that within me, there lives a spirit of the great spirit goddess that someday would be recognized. When I first saw this lady, I asked, "Why me?" I remembered the story of the prodigal son. This time I did not take this story to a priest. I told my son, Floyd, Jr., who believed me.

I started to tell others that White Buffalo Woman is coming back—that the Virgin Mary is coming back when the cherries are black. I kept this up from 1988 to 1994. In March of 1994, about sixty-five people were praying together in Minnesota where I was leading a prayer session, when she appeared. She said when the cherries are black, she would return and her father would take her place. Her father would die, so that she could live. She would come back. She would give us these messages.

Why were the Heiders chosen?

They are humble people. They care about all things. The first Jesus was an avatar—a star person, reincarnated over and over again. Jesus was sent to teach the people. It was important that he was born in a manger with animals. The white buffalo calf also was born in a manger as a woman. She was born to white people—the Heiders—to teach the white people that she was coming back. Miracle was born in the center of the white supremacist area. Now, Miracle brings all kinds of people to this area to show the white people about others.

What does the birth of the white calf mean?

When Miracle came, the Virgin Mary came. One day, the white, black, and yellow man will be morally bankrupt and will come to the Indian. Each of the nations was given a responsibility. The nations which we call the yellow people have the covenant of water—the blood of our body and of mother earth, the rivers, and lakes. The Asian people broke their covenant by raising poppies and making opium. Their form of worship was the yellow stone ball called Buddhism.

The Europeans have the covenant of the air. Their worship was the white stone called the tablet—the Ten Commandments. They broke their covenant by polluting the air with industry, airplanes, and killing the ozone. After their leadership was taken away, they were given the power of creation through machines.

The black people had the covenant of the fire—the energy force. They are supposed to walk in peace, love, and harmony. They broke their covenant by anger. Their worship was the black rock called juju.

The Indian people's covenant was the flesh of the earth mother, the earth. Their covenant was broken too, but the foundation of spirituality was always kept alive by the seven laws, the seven fires brought by the blessed Virgin Mary. She appeared as a white buffalo maiden. The female is sacred. Therefore, you see that the Statue of Liberty is female. The bald eagle is a female. The American flag was created by a female, Betsy Ross.

We are losing our holistic way called common sense. We are at a crucial point in our lives. We are losing the reality of survival. Pollution, the destruction of earth, and overpopulation are killing us. Our value system has changed for thirty pieces of silver.

Dave Heider told me that two eagles came down around him about the time the calf was born. What does that mean?

When the two eagles came, they represented the spiritual people. Twenty-three eagles have come to the Heiders' farm. It means to wake up. Destruction is coming and the eagle is a forewarning sign.

Is there anything else you would like to say about the white buffalo?

Here in our legend, the Indian people must find our place in the ancient culture, not in the modern world. We have forgotten the commonsense, holistic way of life. We are cutting too many trees and warming the earth. Our way of thinking has changed. There is no trust today through computers, no trust of neighbors; all nations are getting very greedy, polluting the water and air.

I have gone from Catholic to Episcopalian and back to Catholic. I went back to the sacred pipe and realized that we are all the same, we are equal, all blood is the same. All different people are coming to the Indian nation to learn the right way because they lost their own culture. I and other Indian people now teach the importance of all life.

HOW RARE IS THE WHITE BUFFALO?

How rare is the white buffalo? How likely is the occurrence of an all-white calf? Are white buffalo as rare today as they were two hundred years ago? From a biological standpoint, these questions are an exercise in rhetoric, for there is no way to know the answers. The great populations of buffalo were gone before anyone had the foresight or the knowledge of genetics to conduct significant scientific inquiry. Massive slaughter decimated the herds, reducing them to the tiniest fraction of their previous numbers in the brief span of little more than two centuries. Any statistical insight into the genetic makeup of the herds was lost with their near extermination. We can make guesstimates based on anecdotal accounts of the period, but the real answer is that we have no answers. What happened to the species was unprecedented.

The numbers of buffalo that once roamed the Great Plains were staggering. Estimates ranged from

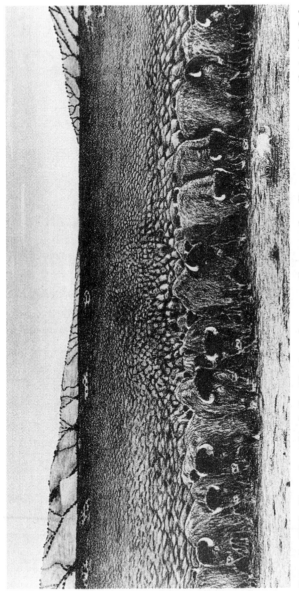

Before the 1830s, bison migrated in herds without number—an endless mass of woolly grazers ranging across the prairie. Only a few decades later, bison were nearly extinct. (Courtesy Kansas State Historical Society, Topeka, Kansas)

a conservative 40 million animals to a high of 70 million. By the 1750s, there were no longer any buffalo east of the Mississippi River; they had all been killed off to make way for settlers. The western plains still teemed with multitudes, however. Accounts by early pioneers spoke of herds so large they blackened the plains as far as one could see, a vast landscape of shaggy beasts grazing on prairie grasses, soothing themselves in mud wallows, and standing impassively against winter storms.

These mighty herds had fed and sustained the Plains Indian tribes for more than ten thousand years. The Indians regularly bartered buffalo robes for tobacco and food crops from other tribes. The buffalo herds were an endless larder for them. With the coming of white traders, the market in buffalo hides increased. Indians traded the robes for forged knives and cooking kettles as well as guns, horses, beads, and alcohol. Traders shipped the robes back east, where they were popular as lap blankets. The lush robes were exported to Europe as well. By the 1840s, hunters were harvesting about a hundred thousand hides per year, an effect that could be seen in the herds.

Railroad lines, laying mile upon mile of tracks across the plains, hired "buffalo runners" to hunt the animals for meat to feed the railway crews. Buffalo Bill Cody, certainly the most famous of the buffalo runners, claimed to have killed 4,280 buffalo in a year and a half. The tracks dissected the buffalo's migratory paths, and the animals split into the northern and southern herds.

Stories of the great numbers of buffalo in the West captured the imagination of the world, and many came to see for themselves. European nobility traveled to the Great Plains for grand buffalo-hunting expeditions. In 1854, Sir Saint George Gore, an Irish lord, embarked on a hunt that lasted almost three years. He took seventy saddle horses, forty servants, and thirty wagons to carry supplies. At night he sipped on vintage wine and slept in a brass bed. The expedition cost some $500,000 and brought down two thousand buffalo.

Sport hunting became the rage. Buffalo Bill guided eastern millionaires as well as the Grand Duke Alexis of Russia. Low-priced excursions were promoted by the railroads. Trains would chug alongside the herds while passengers simply lowered the windows to take aim. Rarely did the trains stop to harvest the kills; the carcasses were left to rot on the plains. The "sport" in this hunting was often called into question, for great beasts simply stood there, picked off en masse by the hunters.

Hunting for sport and meat took a toll on the herds, but it didn't begin to compare to the slaughter that began in the 1870s. A new tanning method had been developed, creating numerous new uses for buffalo. Hides with hair were still used for robes, but hides could be processed into a high-quality, flexible leather that was used for cushions and the tops of carriages and sleighs. Tooled and textured, it was used to panel the walls of dens and libraries in the homes of the wealthy, as was the fashion of the day. The English army replaced many of its standard-issue

This mountain of bison skulls testifies to the huge number of animals killed during the great slaughter. The "second harvest" was the collecting of their bones to be shipped back east and ground into fertilizer. (Courtesy Burton Historical Collection/Detroit Public Library)

cowhide items with buffalo leather because it was highly durable. There was also a large market for buffalo leather in industry, where it was sliced into belts that ran the machinery of the burgeoning Industrial Revolution.

With this new demand for buffalo hides, droves of hunters headed west to make their fortune. The nation was suffering a depression, and many young men saw opportunity on the Great Plains. It was relatively easy to get started: All a man needed was a gun and a horse. The professional hide hunters took teams of tanners with them. The overkill was wanton, as the hunters sometimes downed as many as four animals for every hide harvested. Sometimes they only cut out the tongues, for smoked buffalo tongue was a delicacy in fancy New York restaurants. The plains were littered with rotting carcasses.

The slaughter was staggering. In 1872, the Topeka newspaper reported:

Few persons probably know how rapidly the American bison is disappearing from the Western plains. . . . Some idea of the extent of the ruthless slaughter may be formed from the fact that twenty-five thousand bison were killed during the month of May south of the Kansas Pacific Railroad for the sake of their hides alone, which are sold at the paltry price of two dollars each on delivery, for shipment to the eastern market. Add to this five thousand—a small estimate—shot by tourists and killed by the Indians to supply meat to the people on the

> *frontier, and we have a sum total of thirty thou-*
> *sand as the victims for a single month.*

That was thirty thousand hides for one month, from one depot, in one state. Estimates were based on train manifests, multiplied by the amount of hides that filled a railway car. The numbers were probably a fairly accurate measure of the killing that was taking place all across the plains, from Montana to Texas. By 1874, the southern herd had been decimated. The hide hunters looked north.

A few voices were raised against the slaughter and several laws were proposed, but little progress was made. The government, viewing the extermination of the buffalo as the solution to the Indian problem, chose a path of inaction.

In 1874, two federal bills to save the buffalo were put before the United States Congress; one to protect the buffalo, the other to tax the hides. The proposed hide tax was killed in committee, but the buffalo protection bill actually made it through Congress and was passed by both the House and the Senate. It then went to President Ulysses S. Grant, who pigeonholed the bill on the advice of his western generals. After a year, the unsigned bill became a pocket veto.

The government had decided to starve out the Indians by allowing the slaughter to continue. In fact, it was tacitly encouraged, as army forts gave out free ammunition to the hide hunters. At a joint meeting of the Texas legislature in 1875, General Philip Sheridan was reported to have said: "[The hide hunters] have done more in the last two years and will do more in the next year to settle the vexed Indian question, than the entire regular army has done in the last thirty years. They are destroying the Indian's commissary, and it is a well-known fact that an army losing its base of supplies is placed at a great disadvantage. Send them powder and lead, if you will; for the sake of lasting peace, let them kill, skin and sell until the buffaloes are exterminated."

It was estimated that some five thousand hunters spread across the northern plains, sending trainload after trainload of hides back east. By the 1880s the northern herd had been killed off as well. No one believed that this could have happened, for the numbers of bison had been so large. Even the hide hunters didn't believe it; they thought the buffalo had simply migrated elsewhere, perhaps crossing the border into Canada. But the Canadian herds were gone too. Of the forty million buffalo that had roamed the Great Plains, fewer than a thousand animals remained in the late 1880s. And of those remaining animals, most belonged to private herds; fewer than forty animals could be found in the wild.

A small group of conservationists worked diligently to save the remaining buffalo. Reduced to .000025 percent of its original population, the buffalo was snatched from the brink of extinction. The gene pool very nearly evaporated. The few animals left at the end of the century carried the genes for all future bison.

Genetic data on the great herds do not exist, and the only way to judge the diversity of those herds is through historical accounts. Scientists and explorers of the last century recognized differences in the size, conformation, and color of buffalo, and they used these variables to name subspecies.

A broad generalization can be made that buffalo are usually some shade of brown: Usually a mantle of long, curly, very dark brown or black hair covers the head and front legs; tan or light brown, long, woolly hair covers the hump; and short, dark brown fur covers the rear portion of the animal. In fact, bison exhibit a wide range of colors, from black, red, yellow, pied, and white to combinations thereof (Color Plate 3). Within the original buffalo herds, this wide range of colors and patterns most likely indicated a genetically diverse population. Fur color is not a conservative trait, which means that it changes more rapidly through genetic combinations than do the shapes of bones or teeth. If scientists had been able to study the bison herds of a century ago, they may well have noticed subtle variations in fur color between the southern and northern herds.

A range of colors and patterns is even evident in the earliest human records of bison. Between seventeen thousand and thirty thousand years ago, incredible images of bison and other animals were painted or etched onto the walls of European caves, particularly in what is now southern France. The Ice Age bison documented on these cave walls have a coloration similar to that of bison today: dark heads, legs, and underbellies and a lighter-colored hump. The ancient artists depicted the animals in shades of brown, black, and ocher. Modern archaeologists and art historians do not know how accurately the artists mixed their paints to reflect the true colors of their models, but these colors certainly fall within the range of modern bison. Pattern variations shown in the cave paintings include mostly black bison with small tan areas on the flanks or bison with large light areas and black fringe on the legs, belly, and head. To date, no images of white bison have been found in prehistoric caves.

These Paleolithic paintings show the ancestors of the bison that inhabited the northern regions of Europe and eventually migrated over the Bering Strait land bridge to the New World. A well-preserved specimen of one of these ancestors, *Bison priscus,* was discovered in Alaska, its frozen remains mummified over time. This male bison, named "Blue Babe" because of the bluish mineral crystals that formed on the body, had been attacked and killed by lions, and the upper portion of his body had been eaten by the predatory cats. The kill probably took place late in the season, the winter snow covered

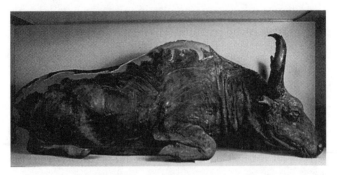

This extraordinarily well-preserved bison ancestor actually died some thirty-six thousand years ago. The bull, known as "Blue Babe," is the most complete Ice Age bison found to date. (Courtesy R. Dale Guthrie)

[1] *Karl Bodmer's painting entitled* Women of the White Buffalo Society *is one of the most striking examples of the ceremonial use of white buffalo hides recorded in the nineteenth century. (Courtesy Joslyn Art Museum, Omaha, Nebraska)*

[2] *The story of White Buffalo Woman (Pte San Win) continues to be a powerful force in the life of many American Indians. The birth of Miracle has been seen as a fulfillment of the promise that she made to the Lakota to return in times of need.* (Buffalo Calf Woman *by Oscar Howe, University of South Dakota Collection,* © *Adelheid Howe, 1982)*

[3] *Modern bison exhibit a wide range of colors, including shades of brown, red, and black. A diversity of color and variety of color patterns have always been evident in North American bison herds. (© DMNH/ Nancy Jenkins)*

[4] *This painted image on a canyon wall in Texas shows a man and a dancing bison or, very likely, another man in a bison cape. The image is possibly a buffalo shaman or impersonator. (© Robert W. Parvin)*

[5] *With a pure white coat and dark eyes and muzzle, Miracle was born on the Heider farm in Janesville, Wisconsin, in August 1994. The birth of a female white buffalo calf, highly revered by Plains Indian tribes, is considered by many to be a prophetic event foretold in Indian myth. (© David and Valerie Heider)*

[6] *Miracle's birth attracted worldwide media attention, and in two years some 75,000 people—both Indian and non-Indian—have visited the Heider farm to see her. (© David and Valerie Heider)*

[7] *Miracle has changed colors four times in the first two years of her life—from white to black (above), to cinnamon red . . .*

[8] *. . . and then yellow (above). Some tribal elders predict she will turn back to white. (Top © Inter-Tribal Bison Cooperative; Bottom © David and Valerie Heider)*

Albinism occurs in most animal species.

[9] *Although uncommon, albino squirrels are found throughout the United States. They have the telltale pink eyes, nose, and light skin that is typical of albinism. (© Deanne D. Cunningham)*

[10] *An albino red-winged blackbird is a rarity. Instead of black feathers, this one has white plumage, and the normally brilliant scarlet patch on the wing is a faded red. (© DMNH/Rick Wicker)*

[11] *An albino buffalo calf was born on the Shirek ranch in North Dakota during the summer of 1996. Note the pink eyes and ivory-colored muzzle and hooves. (© Dan Shirek)*

[12] *Also during the summer of 1996, two partially white buffalo calves were born on the ranch of veterinarian Gerald Parsons in Oklahoma. Both have similar coloration—white legs, underbelly, and throat. (Courtesy Gerald W. Parsons)*

[13] *Since word of Miracle's birth was first mentioned in the media, people have come to pay homage to her, leaving offerings on the gate to her pasture. In the beginning it was just a few small medicine bags (inset) tied to the fence by Native Americans. In the two years since Miracle's birth, the items have included everything from children's toys to Egyptian scarabs. When the first gate was filled to capacity, the Heiders removed it for safekeeping and replaced it with another. Seven gates have been covered with offerings.* (© David and Valerie Heider)

it, and Blue Babe remained there for some thirty-six thousand years. What was remarkable about this specimen was that much of the soft tissue, including muscles, organs, and skin, remained intact. From the hair left on the body, it was possible to reconstruct what Blue Babe looked like. He was dark brown with black points and reddish highlights. Not surprisingly, he resembled the bison depicted on cave walls.

Sadly, no paintings of bison like Blue Babe have been found farther south in the Americas. A few pictographs have been found on canyon walls in the Southwest, but they are rare. Of note, however, is a small painted image in Big Bend National Park in southern Texas (Color Plate 4). It is the most southern image of a prehistoric bison known, although actual bison bones have been found as far south as the state of Chihuahua in Mexico. Another fine image of a bison bull was discovered on a smoking pipe that dates back to about A.D. 1000. The pipe was found in the Chicago area but has

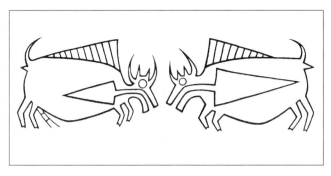

One of the few aboriginal images of bison found east of the Mississippi was engraved on a pipe found in northern Illinois. The pipe is about one thousand years old. (Courtesy Illinois Archaeological Survey)

since been lost, which is truly unfortunate. We could use more evidence regarding the color of ancient bison in the Americas.

Spanish explorer Cabeza de Vaca was the first European to report seeing bison, and he described them as "tawny, some are black." Since that first sixteenth-century account, there have been other descriptions of the color of buffalo, ranging from blue to spotted and from gray to white to pale cream. Exotically colored hides, particularly white ones, commanded higher prices than the more common colors. William T. Hornaday, a zoologist from the New York Zoological Society, studied the buffalo extensively and reported in 1887 that dark brown and light brown were common colors, but that black, gray, and white were also evident.

Early evidence of white buffalo was also recorded by explorers and traders. The first known reference

Early images of bison often looked more like shaggy cattle than real bison. This drawing by Gomara (1554) is the earliest known European depiction. (Courtesy Denver Public Library/Western History Department)

to the white bison was made in 1754 by Antony Henday, a trader with the Blackfoot tribe. He wrote in his journal of seeing a white buffalo hide in an Indian village along the Battle River in Canada. In 1800, explorer Alexander Henry recounted that the Cree had seen a pure-white calf in the midst of a large herd. Edwin James, who recorded Major Stephen Long's expedition to the Rockies in 1819, wrote of seeing pied bison.

Western artist George Catlin estimated that white buffalo were likely "one in a hundred thousand." J. A. Allen, who studied the animals and wrote the most comprehensive nineteenth-century study of bison, estimated that the white buffalo "probably occur in the proportion of not more than one in millions." Using the forty-million figure as the number of buffalo on the plains, Allen's estimate would mean there were only forty white buffalo at any given time. Catlin's estimate would mean there were four hundred. The killing of a white buffalo was considered a newsworthy event, and the *Rocky Mountain News* reported one in Colorado in 1873. After encountering what he thought was a white buffalo, a Colonel Jones of Texas described: "This was the most remarkable phenomenon I had ever witnessed, and for a moment I did not know whether I was awake or dreaming. I had read of the superstition of the Indian in relation to the white buffalo and considered it a phantom—a phantasm of the red man's brain; now I could scarcely believe my own eyes. There the strange animal stood under the noonday sun, chewing its cud—a white buffalo as sure as the world." There is really no way of knowing just how uncommon the white buffalo was or of establishing its statistical likelihood. Suffice it to say that the white buffalo was considered rare even when the great herds still roamed the plains.

Sacrificed by Indians for their powerful spirituality and prized by hunters for the high prices they could command, white hides were a sought-after commodity. White buffalo were shot and killed whenever they were encountered, and their color made them easy targets. This constant pressure kept their numbers low. Hornaday went so far as to say that white buffalo never reached adulthood. Because they were usually killed as calves, it can be assumed that few, if any, reached breeding age.

But what, exactly, is the biological significance of the white bison? For that matter, why should we care about bison fur color at all? The answer lies in the fact that fur color is more than an aesthetic aspect of bison biology; it offers important clues to genetic variation within the species and the animals' adaptability to their environment. For any species, a good degree of genetic variation is necessary to maintain a healthy population. Hair color is an easy form of variation to observe and thereby gauge the genetic diversity of the bison population.

Under natural conditions, hair color may affect an animal's survival. For example, among predator species, such as lions and cheetahs, blending into their environment helps them surprise prey from close range. For predators, surprise often leads to a successful hunt and subsequent survival. For prey species, such as bison, antelope, and other grass eaters, a delicate balance must be maintained. Individuals must look alike to predators but different to each other. Individuality in size, hair color, or horn configuration may confer an advantage in attracting mates or intimidating competitors. However, an animal that stands out from the rest of the herd makes an easy target for predators, and it may not be well received by the herd itself. Although a white buffalo indicates that genetic diversity exists within the species, being white does not seem to be particularly advantageous for the individual.

How then does a buffalo get to be white? There are three explanations. The first is that some of the white buffalo encountered on the plains were probably albinos. Albinism occurs in many animal species—birds, reptiles, mammals (including humans) (Color Plates 9 and 10). It is a recessive color gene that causes the animal to have no pigmentation. Albinos have white fur, feathers, or skin, and their nose and eyes are usually pink. An albino buffalo calf might also have light-colored hooves and horns. Because of the lack of pigmentation in their eyes, albinos usually have poor vision; blindness is common. Their poor eyesight and conspicuous color combine to make these animals easy targets for predators, whether they be wolves, coyotes, or humans. Without doubt, some of the white bison killed on the plains were probably albinos.

The second explanation is crossbreeding, particularly between a white breed of cattle and a bison. Some of the early bison ranchers experimented with crossbreeding. A rancher named C. J. "Buffalo" Jones coined the word "cattalo" for the cattle-buffalo mix that he was developing in Texas in the late 1800s. This genetic experimentation created unusual results.

Because crossbreeding wasn't attempted until after most of the herds were already exterminated, it is unlikely that Indians or hide hunters saw many crossbreeds. Later bison ranchers would forgo the practice of crossbreeding, preferring instead to develop pure bison bloodlines.

More recently, attempts were made to cross bison with Charolais cattle, a French breed with silky blonde or white fur. Charolais crosses with other cattle breeds became popular with cattle ranchers in the 1970s, when ranchers tried crossing the Charolais with Herefords, Black Angus, and other

When bison and Charolais cattle are crossed, the result can look very much like a purebred white bison. Such crosses are not accepted by Indian elders as authentic. (© Arletta Adair)

varieties of beef cattle in order to produce larger animals. This experimentation sometimes produced unexpected and undesirable results, such as big-shouldered calves that had difficulty during birthing. In the West, the light skin and hair of the Charolais made them susceptible to skin irritations and sunburn as they grazed on the hot, treeless plains. Crossing Charolais with other breeds of cattle lost its appeal, but during the past twenty years, bison ranchers have attempted to cross buffalo with Charolais. The result of this crossbreeding can be quite striking, as the animals are often shaped like bison but have the long, white, silky coats of the Charolais. The bulls produced from this mating, however, are sterile. Interest in this type of cross-

Charolais cattle are large beef cattle with silky blonde or white hair. They were imported from France to cross with other breeds of beef cattle. (© Robert B. Pickering)

breeding has again waned, but it explains many of the white bison seen today. Indian elders, however, claim that this kind of white buffalo is not pure, and therefore not sacred.

The third explanation for a white buffalo is the emergence of a recessive, non-albino gene for color. This most likely accounts for the white calf born on the Heiders' farm, although the exact genetic mechanism is not yet known. However, because Miracle's unusual color cannot be explained by the other two theories on white coloring, this seems to be a reasonable assumption.

Miracle does not exhibit the typical pink eyes and muzzle or other characteristics of an albino. In fact, except for her white fur, she has dark features—dark eyes, muzzle, and hooves. It is extremely unlikely that she is a crossbreed, for the Heiders had only one bull at the time and there were no other cattle—Charolais or otherwise—in the vicinity.

From the history of Miracle's dam and sire, no one could have predicted such a special calf. Both the dam and the sire were purchased in 1990. For the first two years, the dam did not produce any offspring and the Heiders considered her for freezer meat. They tried breeding her again, however, and this time she produced a male calf of normal color. The following year, Miracle was born, and the year after that, another female calf with white legs was born. This calf is Miracle's half sister (they have the same mother, but different fathers, as Miracle's father died shortly after her birth), and her coloration indicates that the genetic link for white fur is most likely through the dam.

Perhaps even more unusual than Miracle's white coloring as a calf is her subsequent color change, from white to black to red and now yellow (Color Plates 7 and 8). Because historically, white buffalo calves were killed while still young, it is unknown whether this is typical for white buffalo.

Prior to Miracle's birth, the most famous white buffalo of the century was a bull named Big Medicine. He had blue eyes and was all white except for a crown of dark fur on top of his head. Big Medicine lived for twenty-six years on the National Bison Range in western Montana, where he became quite a tourist attraction. One of the male calves he sired was a full albino.

Another white buffalo was documented in the 1950s—in Alaska, of all places. Mr. and Mrs. Harold Berry discovered this animal living at the U.S. Army

Big Medicine, a partial albino, was the most famous white buffalo before the birth of Miracle. (Courtesy Montana Historical Society, Helena)

Arctic Testing Center at Fort Greely, south of Fairbanks, as part of a herd that had been transplanted
from Montana. This white buffalo, like Miracle, had
brown eyes and a brown muzzle, so it could not have
been an albino. A number of bison in this herd had
white blotches or streaks on their flanks, but only the
one was completely white. Traces of white could
occasionally be found in the coats of some newborn
calves, but these animals did not live long. The white
individual was three years old when the Berrys
encountered him. He apparently did not live more
than a few years after that time.

Other white buffalo have been born in recent
years. Two albino calves were born on the Shirek
ranch near Michigan, North Dakota, in 1996. (The
dams of these two calves were in feedlots with other
young cows and bulls, so the sires are unknown—

*In 1959, Betty Berry photographed this white bison and herd roaming
through the trailer park at the U.S. Army Arctic Testing Center, 107
miles south of Fairbanks, Alaska. (© 1959 Betty Berry)*

sort of the bison equivalent of premature, unplanned pregnancies.) The first calf lived only five weeks, but the second is alive and appears healthy (Color Plate 11). This calf has typical albino coloring, with white fur, pink eyes and muzzle, and horns and hooves of an ivory color. The calf's behavior seems normal, as do its associations with the other bison in its herd. The Shirek family has a herd of about eighty animals and has been raising bison since 1982.

Dan Shirek called Dave Heider to ask what he could expect regarding public reaction to the white buffalo. Dave shared some of his experiences, but couldn't predict what the response would be. Shirek said that only two hundred or so people, mostly from the surrounding area, had come to see the calf, and only about ten of those were Native Americans. The Shireks seemed a little disappointed. Lakota elders, however, have accepted the calf as a sacred white buffalo.

In the summer of 1996, a white calf was born on the Pine Ridge Reservation in South Dakota. The calf's owner also called Dave Heider to ask what to expect in the way of public reaction. He replied, "You're the Indian, not me." Dave Heider is a man of few words, but he is direct. This calf also has been accepted by the Lakota elders as sacred, though again, few people have traveled to see it.

In addition to these white calves, other bison provide evidence of the color variation present in the current buffalo population. Responses to questionnaires that I sent to members of the American Bison Association revealed a surprising range of exotic colors or patterns: a number of completely black animals; several bison with black or dirty white blotches; two cinnamon-colored cows; one calf with a black blotch on the right hip, and another in the same herd with a white blotch on the left hip. Perhaps the most intriguing examples were two partially white bison born in 1996 on the ranch of veterinarian Gerald Parsons, near Stratford, Oklahoma. One calf has white legs, underbelly, and throat—the parts of a bison's body that are usually the darkest (Color Plate 12). The second calf has similar coloration but with a darker back and a strip of nearly black hair along the spine. Both of these calves were sired by the bull that won the 1995 Gold Trophy at the National Western Stock Show in Denver. There aren't any questions about the quality of this bull's bloodlines. However, it would appear that the father

Two bison born on the ranch of Doug Paulson of Medora, North Dakota, exhibit blotchy color variants; one animal shows a black patch of fur and the other presents a dirty white patch on the hip. (Courtesy Doug Paulson)

is the genetic link for the white coloration in these two calves, whereas for Miracle and her half sister, the mother was the link.

Although it is impossible to know the genetic variation of the pre-slaughter herds, it is possible to more closely define the range of genetic variabilities today. This is done through genetic testing. Stormont Laboratories of Woodland, California, works with ranchers to determine the genetic makeup of their herds through blood testing. The North American Bison Registry, founded in 1972, also strives to establish bison bloodlines. The registry was established for the purpose of ensuring the purity of the breed, verifying parentage so that superior bloodlines can be identified, and encouraging the genetic propagation of exceptional stock for breeding programs.

The genetic codes of herds today come from the few buffalo that were still alive at the end of the nineteenth century. It is impossible to increase the quantity of genes inherited from these individuals, but through controlled breeding the number of genetic combinations can be increased.

Virtually all bison now live in managed environments, whether on private ranches or on public parklands. Even at Yellowstone National Park, the bison are not completely free-ranging, but are managed in order to ensure the genetic diversity of the herds. The animals' movements from pasture to pasture are controlled and the size and makeup of the herds are monitored. This is usually accomplished by limiting the breeding opportunities. In ranching, bison herds

are managed to produce the most desirable characteristics, whether the goal be genetic diversity or
juicier steaks.

The task for today's scientists is to determine the
range of genetic diversity within current bison herds.
This information will lead to even greater diversity
through new genetic combinations. Genetic diversity
is vital to all species because it provides a natural protection against disease and ensures the long-term via-
bility of the species. As the number of bison grows, so
do the possible genetic combinations.

So we are back to the question of the rarity of the
white buffalo. In the vast herds that once roamed the
Great Plains, the instances of white buffalo were rare
enough that the Indians worshiped it. Traders also
recognized the value and rarity of the white hide.
Most of these buffalo were probably albino, a more
likely genetic combination than that of a non-albino
white buffalo.

Within a blink of an eye in human history, the
great herds were nearly wiped out, reduced from
forty million to fewer than a thousand animals within
a span of two centuries—with most of the kill-off
occurring during the final twenty years. In the tiny
gene pool that remained was a smaller chance for
the genetic combination that would produce the
rare albino bison. And smaller still was the chance of
the genetic combination that would produce a non-
albino white buffalo. Yet on the Heiders' ranch, into
their herd of just fourteen buffalo, a white calf with
brown eyes was born.

How rare is the white buffalo? Very.

CHAPTER FIVE

BISON RANCHING IN THE NEW WEST

In 1887, zoologist and noted buffalo authority William T. Hornaday wrote about the impending extinction of the bison: "The wild buffalo is practically gone forever, and in a few more years, when the whitened bones of the last bleaching skeleton shall have been picked up and shipped East for commercial uses, nothing will remain of him save his old, well-worn trails along the water-courses, a few museum specimens, and the regret of his fate." This dire prediction ignited public sentiment, particularly in the East, to save the great icons of the West.

Hornaday served as the first president of the American Bison Society, an organization instrumental in buying rangeland as protected habitat for bison. The membership was composed of a small group of dedicated individuals, mostly Easterners who, having read newspaper accounts of the great slaughter that was taking place in the West, were determined to save the bison from extinction. The ABS raised funds, wrote letters, and lobbied the United States Congress.

The emerging conservation movement prompted the legislation to protect the animals. Poaching had become a problem in Yellowstone National Park, where a small remnant herd was supposedly protected. However, it was more profitable to kill the bison and pay the poaching fine. Laws were passed that significantly raised the fine for poaching.

Through the efforts of the ABS and a growing conservation movement, land was set aside specifically for the bison when the National Bison Range was established in western Montana in 1908. The ABS procured breeding animals to stock the new range and to replenish the dwindling herds at Yellowstone. Canada also put aside parkland where

During the early decades of this century, bison were used on American currency and stamps to romanticize the Old West. (© DMNH/Rick Wicker)

the great animals could roam freely without danger of being hunted. Although the task of building the few remaining herds to sustainable and genetically diverse populations was still to come, the buffalo had been saved from extinction.

Public concern over the future of the bison was a key factor in the conservation movement evident at the end of the nineteenth century. There was a growing awareness that the great untamed West was vanishing and, along with it, species and habitats that were an integral part of the national heritage. Early conservationists played an important role in saving the bison. So too did early bison ranchers.

Many colorful characters were associated with the early days of bison ranching. Charles Goodnight was a famous Texas cattle rancher who started building a buffalo herd in the late 1800s. Texas was one of the few places where large numbers of buffalo still roamed freely in the 1860s and 1870s. Just a few years after the end of the Civil War, Goodnight began gathering calves to make a herd.

One technique that proved successful for Goodnight was to chase a mother buffalo and her calf. By maneuvering his horse between the two animals, he could separate them by some distance. The calf would then follow him back to the ranch, where an accommodating cow provided milk for the orphan bison.

Goodnight and his wife both felt that the demise of the buffalo would be a terrible loss for the country, and this was certainly a part of his motivation. He also felt that there was money to be made, and he tried a number of creative angles to turn a profit.

Because buffalo were known to have unpredictable dispositions—a fact that often proved dangerous to man and horse alike—Goodnight reasoned that he could temper the buffalo by crossbreeding them with cattle. Like any good rancher, he knew that crossing two related species with different characteristics would result in a hybrid with the characteristics of both. He was trying to get the best combination of behavior, size, and conformation, but more often than not, Goodnight's experiments failed, instead producing bad-tempered cows and sterile bulls. There wasn't much of a market for either of these.

Next, he tried marketing buffalo products. Goodnight promoted the therapeutic and curative powers of buffalo fat, which, he contended, when made into a medicinal soap, would cure rheumatism. When he couldn't get doctors to endorse his claim, he changed his tactics and started marketing buffalo fat as a machinery lubricant and silver polish. Goodnight remained a valiant booster for the bison.

C. J. "Buffalo" Jones also experimented with crossbreeding buffalo. By mating a female buffalo with a domesticated cattle bull, Jones came up with a mix he called a "cattalo." Bulls born of this type of crossbreeding were usually sterile, a problem that Jones chose to ignore. His purpose in breeding cattalo was to create larger animals with the disposition of domestic cattle. This, he figured, would yield larger and finer-quality buffalo robes. He claimed that a first-generation cross was bigger than either of its parents. Although this was probably true, the greater size that resulted from the "hybrid vigor" of the first-generation crosses diminished with each successive cross.

Pawnee Bill, Buffalo Bill, and C. J. "Buffalo" Jones—real characters of the Old West. Beyond the hype and self-promotion, their lasting contribution was saving bison from extinction by building small herds. (Courtesy Don Fallis)

Jones also tried to "break bison to the harness" and use them to pull wagons. A relentless self-promoter, he was often pictured in a buckboard pulled by "Lucky Knight," a bull that had killed its previous owner. The ensuing publicity—that Jones could tame a buffalo, particularly a killer buffalo—increased his reputation considerably. He was successful with a few animals, but the practice never really caught on as anything more than a stunt. Other people also tried to domesticate buffalo. Some had dreams that one day buffalo would pull plows on the prairie. And though young calves could sometimes be trained to accept a harness, once hitched to a wagon they would go wherever they pleased.

As a young man, Michel Pablo earned his living as a buffalo runner, shooting the animals for their meat to feed the crews building the transcontinental railroad. Not until much later in life did he realize that the buffalo were nearing extinction, a situation to which he had contributed. Pablo wanted to make amends, and he and a partner started to build a herd. They obtained free pasture rights on the Flathead Indian Reservation in Montana, and as their herd steadily grew, they sold buffalo to parks, zoos, and ranchers.

In the early 1900s, Pablo approached the United States Congress with an offer to sell the government seven hundred buffalo to expand the herds already living in protected parklands and preserves. Theodore Roosevelt and other powerful conservationists favored the transaction, but members of Congress objected and blocked the purchase. They didn't feel that buying buffalo was good use of federal money, especially money that came mostly from taxing the eastern states. Pablo then went to the Canadian government. The superintendent of Rocky Mountain Park in Banff, Alberta, recognized the opportunity and lobbied the Canadian parliament to purchase the buffalo. Pablo's entire herd was bought and relocated to Elk Island Park in Alberta.

Michel Pablo had been a buffalo runner in his early adult life. In later years, he felt remorse for the slaughter and, along with Charles Allard, created one of the largest protected bison herds. Eventually it was sold to the Canadian government. (Courtesy Montana Historical Society, Helena)

Scotty Philip was another fascinating character associated with the move to save buffalo from extinction. Born James Philip in Scotland, he came to the United States in his teens to build a fortune. He tried his hand at many occupations, from gold miner to army courier. Ranching proved to be his path to success, and he became one of the wealthiest and most influential ranchers in South Dakota. He raised thousands of cattle on his many ranches and started raising bison as well. By 1904, Philip had a herd of about eighty buffalo.

Perhaps the best-known escapade associated with Philip was the "Bullfight of the Century," a fight between a Mexican fighting bull and an American bison. The event came about after a Mexican dignitary had visited Philip's ranch. During the visit, both Philip and the Mexican dignitary had made exaggerated claims about the abilities of their respective favorite animals. A friend of Philip's suggested that they arrange a contest to settle the dispute. Hearing of this idea through a network of friends, the manager of a bullring in Juárez, Mexico, soon issued a friendly challenge. Word of the contest spread far and wide, and on the day of the event, the bullring was filled to capacity, mostly with Mexicans who looked derisively at the bison bull sitting calmly in the ring.

The Mexican fighting bull pawed and snorted and charged the bison from the side. The bull, however, had never fought a bison before. Fighting bulls pivot and turn on their hind legs; bison pivot on their front legs because of the massive weight of their shoulders and hump. In a blur, the bison spun around and met the Mexican bull head to head. The fighting bull bounced off. The bison stood his ground with little reaction. And so it went each time the fighting bull charged. Finally the fighting bull was on the ground, exhausted from the one-sided battle. The owners of the Mexican bull were embarrassed and enraged. They claimed that the bull was not a good one and wanted to bring in another, meaner bull. In all, two bison bested three Mexican fighting bulls. The men from Philip's ranch returned to South Dakota with more than enough winnings to pay for the trip.

The Bullfight of the Century makes an unforgettable anecdote in the annals of bison history, but Scotty Philip's real contribution to bison ranching

Much to the shock of the Mexican fighting bulls and the rage of their owners, two of Scotty Philip's bison bulls were undefeated in the Juárez bullring in 1907. This was the first and probably the last time such a fight was staged. (Courtesy South Dakota State Historical Society)

was his dedication to pure bloodlines. Unlike many other ranchers of the time, Philip did not like cattle-bison crossbreeds. He culled them from the herd during roundups and sold them for meat. His foresight proved a great asset. Many herds today trace their lineage to Scotty Philip's ranch and his pure-blooded stock. When Philip died in 1911, he owned the largest bison herd in North America, numbering approximately one thousand head.

Philip was a rancher and a businessman, but he was driven by more than just the desire to turn a profit. He had great respect for bison and admired

Bison are an American success story. Not only was their extinction averted, but, through much hard work, they are no longer an endangered species. State, federal, and local parks have been set aside for bison and other wildlife. Increased ownership of rangeland by private ranchers has also contributed to the success. (© DMNH/Nancy Jenkins)

Bison ranchers believe that bison are less destructive grazers than cattle. This photo taken at the Blue Mountain Bison Ranch in Colorado shows the results of selective bison grazing on the far side. On the near side, cattle have almost destroyed all varieties of plants. (© DMNH/ Rick Wicker)

their strength and loyalty. "If a man wants to get a fine lesson in the advantage of 'standing together,' he need only watch a buffalo herd in stormy weather," Philip was quoted as saying. His high regard for the bison is echoed by modern-day ranchers. Most bison ranchers I have met are motivated by more than just the bottom line. They see bison ranching as a way to preserve a national inheritance, at the same time providing an endowment for the future of the species.

Bison ranching is a growing branch of agriculture. There are about 150,000 bison in the United States today; about 80 percent are on ranches where they are raised for their meat, and the rest live in national parks and preserves. The population increases by about 15 to 20 percent annually, though it is minuscule compared with the number of cattle on ranches, where more than a half million animals are slaughtered each week to supply the American dinner table with beef. The Cattlemen's Association need not worry about competition from bison ranchers in the immediate future, but trends indicate that the ratio of beef to bison meat consumed by Americans may be changing. Not only is bison meat more nutritious than beef, but bison ranching is more economically and ecologically sound.

In talking to bison ranchers and members of bison associations, I have found that many hold ideological beliefs in the concepts of sustainable agriculture and minimum impact on the environment. Yes, bison ranching is a business, they have told me, but they also feel strongly about being good stewards of the land. They realize that only a healthy grassland ecosystem will sustain their businesses. Through wise use and minimum-impact ranching, they can maintain the value of this natural resource so that it does not diminish over time. Their concern is threefold: to maintain a healthy environment, which, in turn, will sustain a productive industry well into the future, which, in turn, will preserve the bison. As ranchers like to say, "If you want to save the buffalo, eat more bison." Or, put another way, "No one ever worries about chickens becoming extinct!"

Profit motive and ecological sensitivity are often thought of as antithetical, yet bison ranching is an industry in which the two go hand in hand. This, it seemed to me, was an odd marriage of conservative economics and liberal environmentalism. Environmentalism is often considered part of the "liberal agenda," yet among bison ranchers, a new conservative environmentalism has developed. I asked Paul Jonjak, president of the National Bison Association, about this, thinking that I had hit upon a great but unnoticed truth. "Sure, they're related," said Paul. "That's why I got into bison ranching." So much for my probing insight into the obvious.

The National Bison Association (formerly the American Bison Association), based in Denver, Colorado, is the trade organization of bison ranchers. There are about 2,500 members from Canada to Mexico. (Courtesy National Bison Association)

Paul Jonjak owns the Blue Mountain Bison Ranch near Loveland, Colorado. His land abuts Rocky Mountain National Park, and against a backdrop of majestic, snow-covered peaks, he runs some four hundred bison on 4,500 acres. As much as possible, Paul tries to create a natural range environment, leaving large areas unfenced and allowing the bison to roam freely for most of the year. Although his ranch could support a herd twice the size, Paul has decided to limit the number of bison to avoid over-grazing. He also wants to leave enough forage for the elk and deer that share the range. Paul's chief concern is not to maximize profits, but rather to maintain a healthy habitat while making a good living.

Bison meat is free of the hormones and chemicals frequently used to increase the size and weight of cattle. It has about the same taste as beef but contains less fat and cholesterol. A 3.5-ounce cut of bison steak has 3 grams of fat, 120 calories, and 21 grams of protein, compared with the same-sized piece of beef, which has 14 grams of fat, 210 calories, and 19 grams of protein. Bison costs more per pound, but the greater nutritional value compensates for the higher price.

An economically sound, sustainable agriculture that produces a more healthful meat is reason enough to request the grocery store to special-order it. Yet there is still another, less tangible reason often mentioned by ranchers when they are asked about their motivation for getting into bison ranching. They view the bison as a living and breathing symbol of the Old West, a reminder of the spirit and romance of the frontier. Ironically, bison ranching is not only recapturing the Old West, it is also helping to define the New West.

✦✦✦

Human settlement of the western plains was neither an easy nor a natural transition, but the people came. By 1890, the same year that the Indian Wars came to an end at Wounded Knee, the U.S. Census Bureau declared that the frontier was closed, because the human population density was two or more people per square mile.

The semiarid landscape of the West was not suited for farming. The thin prairie soil was not nearly as rich as the deep, organic, loamy soils of the Midwest, where wheat and corn grew so abundantly that these regions were named the nation's

As more of the West disappears under urban expansion, there is increasing pressure on natural resources, particularly water. (© DMNH/ Photo Archives)

"breadbasket" and the "corn belt." On the western plains, the soils were thin and the rain infrequent. The short-grass prairie was better suited to large-scale ranching than to family farming. Many of the pioneers who tried to eke out an existence on 160-acre homesteads were defeated by the elements. Wave after wave of people left during times of drought. The last major drought, the Dust Bowl of the 1930s, coincided with the Great Depression and saw a mass exodus from the plains states. Today there are fewer people and fewer small towns on the plains than there were in the 1920s.

Agricultural practices have seen dramatic changes as well. As the number of family farms and ranches has dwindled, the land has been bought up and consolidated into corporate megafarms, highly mechanized agribusinesses that employ fewer people. With work difficult to find, the young people pack up and leave for job opportunities in distant cities.

While small rural towns are experiencing outmigration, the major cities of the West are growing. People are moving from the East and West Coasts to escape unemployment, overcrowding, traffic jams, and the high stress of living in more heavily populated and congested urban areas. The populations of cities such as Denver and Phoenix, for example, are growing at unprecedented rates, and so is the resulting urban sprawl, with its associated problems ranging from crime to traffic.

The economic bases are changing as well, with the West seeing a shift away from large-scale extractive industries such as mining, ranching, and farming

and toward high-tech computer and software compa-
nies, telecommunications, and other businesses born
of the Information Age. The raw-material industries,
though still vital to the region, are no longer the
defining economic reality of the West.

These changing economic and demographic
trends, as well as the resulting social and political
ramifications, have led to a new designation for the
region: the New West. Yet, by the very nature of this
rapid change, the New West is difficult to define. It
often seems as much an attitude as a place, holding
the same powerful draw on newcomers today that
the spirit of the Old West inspired in people generations ago. The New West is still considered relatively
unspoiled, a place where opportunities abound and
where the future is being shaped. The romantic ideal
of the Old West has metamorphosed into that of the
New West.

Planners and politicians are watching these
trends and trying to respond to them. New ideas
about what the West should be are coming from surprising places. Two professors from Rutgers University in New Jersey have been studying the changes
taking place, and they have identified numerous—
and startling—social currents affecting the region.

Frank and Deborah Popper began their investi-
gation of the Great Plains in the mid-1980s as an
academic exercise. Frank, a regional and urban
planner, and his wife, Deborah, a geographer, have
sorted through mountains of statistical data and
census information on the West. By examining the
demographics of the region, its transportation

infrastructures, climate, economic bases, and numerous other factors, they created computer profiles that track the social changes now reshaping the West. Then they took their thinking a few steps further. They looked at the region in a larger context, taking into account what had worked—or more importantly, what hadn't worked—as the region was settled over the last 150 years. They combined this information with their computer profile and noticed the convergence of a number of trends. The Poppers then made some very interesting projections on the future of the New West.

They found that a century of agriculture had depleted western soils. In response to this, more and

Frank and Deborah Popper, of Rutgers University, proposed the "Buffalo Commons" concept to end some of the most destructive land use practices. It called for letting large sections of the deep prairie revert to grassland and reintroducing bison. (© Frank and Deborah Popper)

more fertilizers were applied. As large-scale corporate agribusinesses took over, farming methods became more intensive, taking an even greater toll on the land. In addition, the farming of endless square miles of crops in a semiarid environment meant that massive irrigation was needed, which consumed enormous amounts of water, a precious commodity in the West. The Ogallala aquifer, a vast underground water reserve, was slowly being siphoned off. The Poppers contended that farming was, is, and will be poor use of the western plains.

Cattle ranching has also exacted a toll. The prairie landscape is a very fragile ecosystem, one that is easily damaged. Beef cattle, introduced by Europeans, tend to overgraze, eating everything in their path and leaving only a stubble of prairie grasses. Bison are more selective grazers, eating only certain plants, thus leaving behind a diversity of plant species to reseed the plains.

Bison are more naturally suited to the plains. After all, they evolved as the prairie itself evolved. Bison are more physically able to survive the hot, dry summers and the cold, windy winters. They have existed in this environment for tens of thousands of years, a time during which the prairie grasslands flourished.

When the pioneers first came west, they saw an endless sea of grass, the rich tapestry of plant species that made up the prairie. Settlers plowed the sod to plant crops. Ranchers built up the cattle herds that would become the ranching industry, often grazing more cattle per acre than the land could support. The prairie ecosystem disappeared. The bits of native prairie left today are set aside in nature preserves or, ironically, are growing wild in pioneer cemeteries.

From a purely economic standpoint, bison are cheaper to raise than cattle. Essentially undomesticated, bison still manage to give birth on the plains as they have for centuries, pretty much fending for themselves. Cattle, on the other hand, usually require more human intervention, particularly during birthing, which translates into lots of additional work and expensive veterinary bills. In addition, cattle are frequently crossbred for desired characteristics, and this genetic tampering sometimes creates new problems that require medical attention. Costs rise each time an animal is handled by humans, and cattle demand more attention than bison.

Bison are cheaper to raise and more ecologically suited to the plains. Viable herds, however, need large unfenced areas in which to roam. After analyzing maps and computer data on population shifts in the West, the Poppers offered an intriguing proposal. Called the "Buffalo Commons," it outlined a plan according to which the federal government would buy up huge tracts of land and repopulate the areas with native bison.

When the Poppers suggested this idea nearly a decade ago, it prompted a loud outcry from the West. What about the people? was the resounding response. What about our communities, our schools, our way of life? The Poppers explained that their concept for the Buffalo Commons would not include all of the West. They had narrowed it down to areas experiencing the most dramatic decrease in population and loss of economic bases—and with little hope of reversing the downward trend.

The area the Poppers mapped out included 110 counties in 10 western states, home to approximately 400,000 people (out of 6.5 million inhabiting the plains states). Over the next forty years, the Poppers proposed, these areas—totaling nearly 140,000 square miles—could be purchased by the government and allowed to revert to prairie, where, once again, the buffalo would roam. This free-range Buffalo Commons would encompass much of the western Dakotas, western Nebraska, and eastern Montana as well as good-sized portions of Oklahoma, Kansas, and Texas, and parts of Colorado, New Mexico, and Wyoming.

What the Poppers suggested was nothing short of revolutionary. Some Westerners considered it treason. No matter how well reasoned and supported by fact the Poppers' concept was, it had hit an emotional nerve. As public attention focused on their Buffalo Commons proposal—mostly through newspaper articles and letters to the editor pointing out how preposterous the idea was—interest swelled. And so did emotions.

Above all, the Poppers had embarked on their analysis of the West as an intellectual exercise. No one was paying them to do it, nor was it part of their academic duties. They were not out to make policy; they had simply wanted to stimulate healthy debate about the future of the West. It quickly turned into much more. People wanted to know where the heck these Easterners came off telling Westerners how to run things. The mail poured in, stacking high in the Poppers' home and university offices.

The Poppers felt it was important that people not misunderstand what they were proposing, and they wanted to explain their research and why they had reached these conclusions. They made a number of trips to the West, crisscrossing the plains, speaking in school auditoriums and church halls. On at least one occasion, the local sheriffs felt that armed security was necessary. Fortunately, there were no violent incidents. But there was certainly a healthy—and heated—debate. The Buffalo Commons was a startling idea regarding the future of the New West, and it raised a lot of western hackles.

Ten years later, however, there is a surprising twist to this story. It appears that the plains are reverting to buffalo grazing grounds after all—and faster than expected. Even more surprising, it is almost entirely the result of the private sector—not the government—investing in bison ranching operations. The reason for both of these changes is a simple one: money.

It was market economics, not the wild prognostic theories of two East Coast academic elitists, that spurred these changes. The idea of the Buffalo Commons, initially and quite vocally rejected by independent Westerners, was happening naturally. Perhaps it is a self-correction of sorts, a leveling of the ecological and economic scales to a balance more in line with what works best in the plains environment.

The number of bison ranchers is increasing every year. In fact, there are bison ranches in every state in the country, a considerable expansion of the animals' original range. The National Bison Association, which merged with the American Bison Association in 1995, has nearly 2,500 members. The NBA lobbies for bison-ranching legislation, supports research on bison-related issues, and promotes education about bison, the healthful qualities of bison meat, and the advantages of bison ranching over cattle ranching. The association also works with the Canadian Bison Association and the Inter-Tribal Bison Cooperative.

With more than thirty member tribes, the Inter-Tribal Bison Cooperative assists Indian tribes in establishing their own herds and helps those with existing herds to expand them. Reservations are often the recipients of bison that have outgrown national parks. Excess animals from Custer State Park in South Dakota—a herd that originated from sixty animals sold to the park by Scotty Philip in the early twentieth century—are regularly given to various Sioux Indian tribes who run buffalo herds on their reservations.

For Indians the return of the buffalo means more than economic progress; it is a spiritual connection to their past. Many see the birth of the white buffalo calf on the Heiders' farm as a portentous symbol of this connection. And, in a sense, Miracle could also be seen as a symbol of the emerging identity of the New West. Her birth brought bison to the forefront of public attention. Bison ranching, an industry born of a species saved from extinction, is growing and prospering. Bison are a resurgence of the Old West that may well be shaping the future of the New West.

I think back to a story an archaeologist friend of mine told me. A few years ago, he and his wife were in the backyard of their home in Washington, D.C., conducting archaeological experiments. They were cutting bison bones with stone tools and examining the kinds of marks the tools made. A neighbor boy was looking over the fence at their obviously weird behavior, and he asked what the bones were. "Buffalo," they replied. The boy shook his head. "No they're not," he said. "Buffalo are extinct."

In the next decade or so, no child will make that statement. Not only are bison not extinct, they are making a comeback. Chances are, a few years from now, that same boy will be ordering a buffalo burger to go with his milk shake and fries.

CHAPTER SIX

RETURN TO THE HEIDERS' FARM

A lot has changed on the Heiders' farm in the two years since the birth of Miracle, but in many ways things are the same. A welcoming committee of cats still greets people on the front porch, and the dogs, both inside the house and out, still keep an eye on strangers. Ducks, geese, and chickens have the run of the yard, as usual. Dave and Val look the same, and the family and neighbors still pitch in when needed to help them cope with all the visitors who continue to visit the farm to see Miracle. Dave and Val have adjusted to all the changes, for they know that their life will never be the same as it was before the small white buffalo calf was born. At first, they dreaded all of the people, Val told me, and missed the daily routines of their lives. Now, when it's too quiet, they get bored.

I returned to the farm on a cold, snowy day in early November 1996. After having doughnuts and hot tea at the kitchen table, Val and I walked up to the new gift shop and museum—a major change from two years ago. The gift shop isn't large, just a couple of hundred square feet of cement slab with aluminum walls and roof. It's the kind of simple yet functional building that blends into a working farm.

Doris, Val's mother, smiled at us from behind the counter. Display cases held Miracle sweatshirts and T-shirts, coffee mugs, and lapel pins. A large bronze sculpture of Miracle and her mother sat atop a case near the middle of the room. The price tag read $4,500—the most expensive piece in the room. Other cases held the widest selection of buffalo jewelry, fetishes, and carvings that I had ever seen in one place. Although most of the items were commercially manufactured, a good number of pieces were handcrafted by Indian artisans.

Alongside the sales floor is the museum, an alcove set aside to display some of the thousands of offerings, gifts, and tokens left behind by the people who have come to see Miracle. From the very beginning, people left all kinds of things on the gate to the buffalo pasture (Color Plate 13). When the gate became so crowded with offerings that no more would fit, the Heiders removed it and put up a new one. In the two years since Miracle's birth, seven gates have been

The care and feeding of Miracle is partially supported by sales at a small store and museum on the Heiders' farm. The design on this lapel pin has been reproduced on other sale items. (Rick Wicker photo)

covered with offerings. The Heiders decided to keep the gates and offerings intact. As each one filled, they unhinged it, wrapped it in plastic, and stored it in the barn. The very first gate is on display in the museum.

Many of the objects left on the gate are related to American Indian tradition. There are pipes, arrowheads, and feathers among the wide assortment of offerings. All sizes and styles of medicine bags hang from the fence gate. Some are plain leather, others are fringed, and still others are embellished with fancy beadwork. The contents of each bag are known only to the person who left it, though the bags usually contain items imbued with spiritual, magical, or healing powers.

Tobacco is a traditional gift in Indian culture, and in a nod to modern times, people have left packs of cigarettes at the gate. Indian jewelry adorns the fence—a few old pieces of silver and turquoise mixed with more contemporary styles. There are beaded necklaces and earrings, as well as ones made of bone and porcupine quills. Strips of cloth in the sacred colors—yellow, blue, red, and white—are knotted together and tied to the fencing. Even more common are dream catchers, rawhide webs that purportedly let good dreams through and capture bad dreams in their snares. I saw a military-style shoulder patch with tribal insignia and the words "Red Thunder." A dark-skinned, big-eyed plastic doll wearing a beaded buckskin dress has a note attached to her that reads, "To Pte Ska Winyele and our Miracle," left by a woman who had traveled from Ontario to see the white buffalo.

Poems, written by people of all ages and backgrounds, have been left behind for others to read—or perhaps for no one to read. Brief notes thanking Miracle for coming into the world are folded and placed in cracks in the fence posts. There are buffalo nickels and Indian head pennies. Many of the personal items likely have a spiritual connection known only to the people who left them, such as the World War II Marine Corps medal I noticed in one of the museum cases. There are Egyptian scarabs, crystals, and polished stones of different kinds. Some items seem to defy explanation; one man left the title for a Chevy pickup truck. Another fellow didn't have anything to leave, so he helped Dave unload two wagons of hay.

The Heiders themselves have been given gifts, from Indians and non-Indians alike. They have received more than a dozen wool blankets from various tribes, as well as beautiful ribbon shirts and many fine examples of custom-made Indian jewelry. A piece of turquoise, as large as a fist and wrapped in the four sacred colors, arrived by mail. The Dalai Lama, the spiritual leader of Tibetan Buddhism, visited the farm and personally presented Dave with a delicate white silk scarf.

The Heiders have received numerous pieces of art depicting buffalo—particularly Miracle—rendered in bone, plaster, stone, and various other media. One of my favorites is a shiny silver buffalo in a globe of water. When shaken, silver sparkles shower down on the buffalo. It's just like the snow globes I had as a little boy.

Although some of the gifts are of museum quality, others fall into the category of kitsch, such as the bright red tie with a white buffalo that seems to cry out for a loud sport coat. The crew of *Unsolved Mysteries* gave out souvenir ball caps and lapel pins when they came to film. I wondered if Dave and Val had ever worn them.

For nearly two hours, Val and her father, Jerry, gave me a tour of the many items displayed in the cases and attached to the gate. They told me stories associated with particular pieces. Although some were funny, most of the stories were serious, even tragic. As I was looking at the many items, I noticed two children's toys covered with soot. Jerry suggested to Val that she tell me the story of the toys. But she couldn't; it touched her too deeply. Jerry told me the sad story instead.

A woman had brought the two toys, a little white teddy bear and a Bert doll, of Bert and Ernie fame from *Sesame Street*. She had been burned over much of her body and most of her hair had been singed off. Her family had been planning to come and see the calf, but just before their trip, their house caught fire and her two young sons were killed. She had taken pictures of the boys a few days earlier, and the film was at the photo shop when the fire broke out. She came to the farm so that she could send the two stuffed animals to the spirit world to be with her sons. The pictures of two smiling young boys were propped next to the stuffed animals.

Even hearing the story again made Val emotional. She knows that people regard Miracle as a spiritual being, but now there was a new twist: People had started bringing pictures and mementos of the dead. There is a color photo of a beautiful young Indian girl dressed in a fancy dance outfit. Shortly after the photo was taken, the girl, only sixteen years old, was killed in a car accident. A woman dying of cancer came with a number of mementos. She brought a picture of her mother, who had been killed during a mugging; her father's police cap; a baby picture of herself; and a family photo. She claimed that she wasn't looking for a miracle to save her life; her visit was a pilgrimage.

The grief of another family ended up as an unexpected blessing for Dave and Val. A local Janesville woman was mourning the death of her daughter when she heard about Miracle and the death of Marvin, Miracle's sire. Without Marvin, the Heiders' small herd was lacking a bull. She felt that while the loss in her own family could never be replaced, she could at least help Dave and Val complete their bison family, so she bought them a bull to replace Marvin. The cost of a bull can range from $3,000 to $6,000, and its value in building a strong and healthy herd is even greater. Dave and Val were both surprised and touched by her generosity.

Miracle has become a symbol of peace and understanding, and at the same time, her home has become a hallowed shrine. As I looked over all the mementos in the cases and attached to the gate, it reminded me of another place: the Vietnam Veterans Memorial in Washington, D.C. Those black granite walls with more than fifty thousand names engraved in them evoke a similar response. It too is a powerful place that releases deep emotions. Perhaps there are special places in this world, and their importance lies not in where they are located, but in the fact that people were there and left something behind to be remembered, or to commemorate someone. Like placing a small pebble at a roadside shrine, it is an act that is both personal and public—private, yet also meant for all future travelers who walk the same path.

Dave moved an old wooden picnic bench into the museum so that visitors could sit and rest or just spend a few moments by themselves to contemplate the offerings and what they might mean. Some people are so overcome with emotion they stay only a brief time, saying that the objects are too powerful and that they can't remain in their presence for long. Other people stand and look from a respectful distance, and still others walk right up for a closer look, wanting to inspect each one, as if looking closely could lead to a better understanding. Behind a quarter inch of glass are a thousand personal, deeply felt stories.

Knowing why people leave such objects would be interesting, but Dave and Val don't ask. This is part of their nature and it is their gift to their guests. They allow anyone who wishes to come to the farm and participate in the occasion, but they don't judge. It isn't that they aren't interested, but they know that seeing Miracle is a very personal experience and they choose to respect people's privacy.

Leaving the gift shop, I noticed some of the other changes that had occurred in the past two years.

Jerry now has a golf cart to drive back and forth to the pasture. In the winter, it has a plastic canopy that offers some shelter. As we stepped into the cart to go see Miracle, Jerry handed me a parka. The weather in Wisconsin was colder than I had expected. The thermometer reading was at just below freezing, and with the windchill it felt more like zero. Jerry said that the last person to borrow the parka was a young woman on the *Unsolved Mysteries* crew who had flown in from California dressed more for the beach than for a fall day in Wisconsin. It had been warm when I'd left Denver, and I had made the same mistake.

Dave drove by in a front-end loader, and Jerry laughed, calling it "Dave's new toy." He uses it to haul silage and hay up to the bison and to do some of the other heavy work around the farm. New and more efficient equipment has helped the Heiders cope with their additional work and diminished time. There are new electric fences around the three bison pastures, needed as much for the safety of the visitors as for keeping the bison confined. Bison are unpredictable animals and may charge if people get too close.

We arrived at the first pasture, where a young cow and a bull had the place to themselves. Although I knew she was no longer white, I wouldn't have recognized Miracle if Jerry hadn't pointed her out. She was considerably darker, similar in color to the other bison in the herd, but with a cinnamon cast. The long, woolly hair on her hump was slightly golden, almost a blonde color, and she didn't have the dark fringed fur on her legs like the other bison. Jerry and

I stood by the fence to look at Miracle and her "bull friend." If nature takes its course, she should calve for the first time in the spring of 1997.

In the next pasture, heifers and young bulls grazed peacefully. One or two raised their heads to look at us, but they were clearly more interested in eating than in people-watching. A number of them are Miracle's half siblings, and it appeared as if some of them also had a light, blondish coloring on their humps. The spring and summer of 1997 will be a very interesting time for returning to the farm to see what colorations are evident in the newborn calves.

Miracle's mother is in the third pasture, along with the other mature cows and the herd bull. She is the dominant cow once again, no longer assuming the lesser role she had when she stayed at the back of the herd, protecting her newborn calf from public scrutiny. Now when she wants to eat, all the other cows move out of her way.

As Jerry and I walked along the fence, I saw more tokens and offerings. People hang them not only on the gate, but all along the fence and even on trees along the edge of the pasture. When we turned the corner to walk along the back side of the field, there were still more. Jerry, sounding like a professional tour guide, told me what the different offerings meant, when they were put there, and who left them. Some Native Americans prefer to find more secluded places to hold their ceremonies and rituals, he said, and they would come back there for privacy.

People sometimes bury things next to the fence as well. Dave and Val are pretty open about letting people worship or contemplate in their own way, as long as it doesn't endanger the animals or other people, and as long as the rituals don't involve illegal substances. The Heiders are strongly opposed to drugs. It doesn't matter if visitors contend that hallucinogens or other drugs are integral to their religious rites; the Heiders are very clear on this issue: They just say no.

I've talked to Dave and Val a number of times since Miracle's birth, and each time I am amazed at how well they have adjusted to the changes in their lives. They are still the same people, hardworking and plainspoken. Dave still works for the county, but Val has given up her day job to attend to the farm and all the visitors. They seem calmer than they were when I first met them, when they were still reeling from the initial shock of attention and publicity. Now they seem to take everything in stride. They talked comfortably about their last conversation with Ted Turner; spending New Year's Eve with rock star Ted Nugent; and having the Dalai Lama, the governor of Wisconsin, and well-known authors and news reporters drop by. Some of the celebrities they like, and others they tolerate.

On Saturdays and Sundays in the summer, as many as 150 people a day visit the farm. Some days there may be only one or two Native Americans; other days there may be as many as forty. Indians and non-Indians alike continue to come to the Heiders' farm. Parents bring their children and make a day of it, though the youngsters are often more interested in chasing the ducks and geese than they are in seeing a sacred buffalo. All manner and all ages of people still come, from sightseers to psychics, medicine men to Methodist ministers, New Agers to old-timers. The Heiders accept everyone. Witches and channelers have signed the guest book, and even a man claiming to be Jesus Christ. Dave says Jesus drives a nice Cadillac.

Dave estimated that over the past two years, some seventy-five thousand people had visited the farm, coming from as far away as Russia, Australia, Japan, South Africa, and the Middle East. For those who cannot travel to Wisconsin, there are three Web sites— White Buffalo, Miracle, and Beloit Daily News— where anyone with access to the Internet can learn the most recent news about Miracle.

The story continues to receive international coverage in the print and broadcast media. It seems to appear in waves, Dave told me. First, a new article will be published in an American paper, which is picked up by one of the news services and flashed around the world. Then a reporter from another country calls, does an interview, and so it goes. Whether international publicity leads to spiritual superstardom is debatable, but Miracle's name has been mentioned at major ecumenical events, such as the inter-denominational World Day, which was held in Jerusalem in June 1996. Dave and Val do not promote Miracle for such events; her fame seems to be self-generating.

One of the most unexpected aspects of this whole adventure, according to Val, is the fame that she and Dave have achieved. People recognize them even when they are away from the farm or outside of Janesville. They find it embarrassing and somewhat humorous when people tell them how famous they are. Some people even ask for autographs.

Fame notwithstanding, Dave and Val have managed to adjust to their new situation. Not given to hyperbole, Dave claims that there have been some inconveniences, but no big problems really. They are used to the crowds now. The only anger I have heard in his voice was when he spoke of people who don't seem to be able to read signs or tell time. Although the days and times for visitation are clearly posted, there are people who nevertheless feel free to walk into the yard at all hours, even at night. It's hard to live a normal family life and also take care of the farm and the animals when people come traipsing through anytime they want. It's not much fun for the Heiders to turn people away, and it's not much fun for the visitors who are asked to leave.

Dave said he is better at controlling his temper and has learned to read people better. "You can tell pretty quickly if the person is a true believer or just blowing smoke," he told me. "In either case, you have to take them at face value."

From the details of their daily routine to how they see the world, the Heiders' lives have changed in dramatic ways. There are the practical matters of crowds, security, and increased workload, for instance. Their neighbors still help out when needed, a show of community support that has not changed over the past two years. Friends and family have become accustomed to the crowds and the interruptions, but they also take pride in seeing Janesville in the news and on the map. It's the kind of community spirit that is highly valued in the Midwest, the salt-of-the-earth attitude that city dwellers lament as missing from urban life. A sense of community is strong here.

The Heiders have never exploited the calf for financial gain, and they don't intend to. They don't charge a fee for seeing Miracle. But the reality of the situation is that they have more expenses now than before the calf was born. The revenue generated by the gift shop helps offset the added expenses. Dave and Val are practical people, and they know that tourists will be tourists. People want to buy a souvenir to take home whether they're visiting Mount Rushmore or the shrine at the Lourdes grotto.

People often make voluntary donations, sometimes substantial ones, but the large sums of money have not come rolling in as some had predicted early on, and Dave and Val do not solicit funds. They are considering other ways to make money to cover expenses, and their plans include increasing the size of the herd and maybe even selling bison meat.

Miracle certainly offers the potential of great wealth. The Heiders are still approached by people and groups who want to buy Miracle. One Indian tribe—Dave won't reveal which one—offered a trade of 750 head of buffalo, valued at more than $2.5 million. Dave and Val received an even larger offer from one of the country's major bison-ranching outfits. Book and movie deals have been broached as well. If they wanted to, Dave and Val could easily take the money and just walk away from all the hoopla surrounding the white buffalo. Instead they politely decline the offers. It isn't that they wouldn't like to be rich, but they know they have a responsibility, and they believe that what they are doing is a service to humanity. The Heiders see Miracle as a spiritual gift to the world and feel a personal obligation to protect and care for her, as well as to share this gift with others.

A few months before my visit, Floyd Hand, the Lakota elder who prophesied both the birth of Miracle and the death of Marvin, had come to the farm to pay homage to Miracle on her second birthday. Before his trip, I spoke to Floyd by phone and there was excitement in his voice, the excitement of a pilgrim readying himself for an important journey. I asked him if there was even more to his prophecy about Miracle. Although he would not elaborate, he said that the prophecy would continue to unfold, that there would be still more changes in Miracle, and that her importance would continue to grow. And, I remembered, there is still his prediction about the twenty-first day of the twenty-first year of the twenty-first century—when the world will live in harmony.

I asked Floyd how well he thought Dave and Val had coped with the many changes they have had to face, with having their lives turned upside down. He quickly corrected me. "Their lives were not turned upside down," he said. "They were chosen." His meaning was clear. From his perspective, the birth of Miracle was not a trial to endure; instead, it was an honor bestowed.

Dave has spoken with the elders of various tribes who revere the white buffalo. I asked him if there have been other predictions regarding Miracle. He said yes, but he prefers not to discuss them. Just as Dave and Val have decided not to ask about or judge the motivations of the many people who have come to see Miracle, they do not discuss the sacred knowledge given them in confidence by tribal elders. Perhaps because of their discretion as well as their custodianship of Miracle, they have been honored by being inducted into the Lakota tribe at Pine Ridge.

Native American spirituality reflects an evolving, highly adaptive perspective on the world. Even within the two years since Miracle was born, there had been a change in outlook. Traditionally, a white buffalo would have been sacrificed, its hide and horns and skull used for ceremonial purposes. In fact, members of the White Buffalo Society did approach the Heiders about sacrificing the calf. But tribal elders, as well as Dave and Val, were against it. Is this simply a reflection of the politically correct nineties? Or is it another example of the continuing evolution of Native American thought? These are interesting questions to ponder. Even the elders, medicine men and women, and tribal leaders are waiting to see how the story of Miracle will unfold.

And where does Miracle fit into the larger scope of human spirituality? What does she represent to the thousands of non-Indians who have made a pilgrimage to Janesville, Wisconsin? They have stood at the fence to gaze at the white buffalo. What exactly they are looking for only they know, but indeed, everybody seems to be looking for something—perhaps a sign, an epiphany, or a deeper understanding of the sacredness of the white buffalo; perhaps a deeper understanding of their own spirituality.

In some cases, seeing Miracle has changed people's lives. Dave remembers a Catholic priest who renounced his priesthood at the gate to the pasture. He wondered how a buffalo could have such a profound effect. Would the priest have renounced his vows anyway? Was he looking for an appropriate place that was spiritual yet not necessarily Christian? Or does Miracle hold some special power that is felt by the people of many religions?

To me, one of the most important parts of this story is the personal journey experienced by each person who sees Miracle. I think of them as the seekers and the believers. The seekers are searching for something, although they may not know exactly what. They may be looking for a sign that will change their lives, an aura, or a communication of some sort from Miracle that signifies her sacredness. They may leave with a feeling of inner peace, or they may leave feeling nothing at all. Some seekers leave disappointed. What they see is not what they are looking for. No longer white, Miracle is now harder to pick out among the other buffalo. If she is not white, they think, then perhaps she is not sacred either. They walk away, still seeking.

The believers are a different matter. For them the changes in Miracle's color validate the story of the White Buffalo Woman and the prophecy it tells. At the end of the story, the White Buffalo Woman changed color four times, from black to brown to red to white. For those who come to the farm believing in the prophecy, this confirms that Miracle is special, that she is truly a sacred being, for she too changed to four colors—from white to black to red to yellow. The believers usually stay to pray or to leave offerings.

Although Dave and Val have made the decision not to ask people about the nature of their beliefs, the anthropologist in me wishes that they would—or that I could. As an anthropologist, I strive to put small events into larger contexts. I try to see patterns and compare different versions of the same story to learn what is at its core. When it comes to spirituality, however, an analytical perspective is difficult to apply. Each person has his or her own view of the world, and scientific logic doesn't always factor in. Perhaps it is as Joseph Campbell says: "Each religion is true, in its own time and context."

I have often thought that places of spiritual power are mirrors in which we see reflections of ourselves. Whether at the cathedral at Chartres, a small church with wood-plank floors in northern Mexico, or the Heiders' farm, we come to look in the mirror to see who is looking back. The attitude—the openness—that we bring determines whether the mirror is obscured in smoke or the reflection gives us new insight into ourselves and the surrounding world.

I asked Dave where he and Val stood in relation to the believers and the seekers. Has Miracle changed their spiritual views? Dave became quiet for a moment. Clearly, this is something he had thought about. He replied that they are still in the middle, that they have not formed any conclusions. He is often asked if he can feel the power of the calf. He claims that he can't. Dave knows something happens to many of the people who come to see Miracle, but it hasn't happened to him or Val.

Arval Looking Horse, keeper of the sacred buffalo pipe and perhaps the most important spiritual leader among the Lakota, has come to the farm on several occasions. During one of these visits, he and Dave stood at the fence looking at the calf. Dave asked him, "Is that the real thing?" Arval Looking Horse responded with a question of his own: "What do you see?" Dave didn't have an answer.

My reaction is very much the same. Much of what has happened I simply do not understand. I do not know how Floyd Hand could have predicted the things that have come to pass. I do not know how—or why—so many people, both Indian and non-Indian, are deeply affected by the spiritual significance of the white buffalo. The skeptic in me remembers too many other events that were supposed to bring peace and harmony. I recall the Age of Aquarius and the Harmonic Convergence. At a lecture almost twenty years ago, I heard a Mexican woman say that the discovery of the great Coyolxauhqui Stone, depicting the Aztec goddess of the moon, during subway excavations in Mexico City would usher in a time of enlightenment and brotherhood among all people. If it did, I missed it.

Nevertheless, there are certain patterns and trends that have coincided with the birth of the white buffalo. The buffalo herds are returning to the Great

Plains. Social and economic changes are reshaping the region, now redefined as the New West. There is a resurgence of American Indian culture and spirituality. And perhaps on another level, the birth of the white buffalo signifies an awakening of spirituality in all peoples, a collective need to reconnect to the earth and to seek deeper meaning in an increasingly technological world. For some people, Miracle is the cause; for others, she is the effect.

One more time I stand at the Heiders' fence and look across the pasture at Miracle. She has changed much since I first saw her as a small white calf two years ago. The fact that she is no longer white doesn't bother me. I know she is special. I think back to the question Dave Heider asked Arval Looking Horse: "Is that the real thing?" There are many ways of seeing the white buffalo. I know what I see. What you see is up to you.

SUGGESTED READING

GENERAL BOOKS AND ARTICLES

Barsness, Larry. *The Bison in Art: A Graphic Chronicle of the American Bison*. Flagstaff, Ariz.: Northland Publishing, in cooperation with Amon Carter Museum of Western Art, 1977.

———. *Heads, Hides, and Horns*. Fort Worth: Texas Christian University Press, 1985.

Dary, David A. *The Buffalo Book*. Newbury Park, Calif.: Sage Books, 1989.

Gruenau, Douglas. *Bison: Distant Thunder*. New York: Takarajima Books, 1995.

Hodgson, Bryan. "Buffalo: Back Home on the Range." *National Geographic,* November 1994, 64–89.

Inman, Col. Henry. *Buffalo Jones' Forty Years of Adventure*. Topeka, Kans.: Crane and Company, 1899.

Lee, Wayne C. *Scotty Philip: The Man Who Saved the Buffalo*. Caldwell, Idaho: Caxton Printers, Ltd., 1975.

Matthews, Anne. *Where the Buffalo Roam*. New York: Grove Weidenfeld Press, 1992.

Stanford, Dennis. "Bison Kill by Ice Age Hunters." *National Geographic,* January 1979, 114–119.

SCHOLARLY BOOKS AND ARTICLES

Allen, Joel Aseph. *The American Bisons: Living and Extinct*. Memoirs of the Museum of Comparative Zoology, vol. 4, no. 10. Cambridge, Mass.: Harvard University Press, 1876.

Frison, George C. *The Wardell Buffalo Trap 48 SU 301: Communal Procurement in the Upper Green River Basin, Wyoming.* Anthropological Papers No. 48, Museum of Anthropology, University of Michigan. Ann Arbor, 1973.

Guthrie, R. Dale. *Frozen Fauna of the Mammoth Steppe.* Chicago, Ill.: University of Chicago Press, 1990.

Hornaday, William T. "The Extermination of the American Bison." In *Annual Report of the Smithsonian Institution, Part II,* 367–548. Washington, D.C.: Government Printing Office, 1887.

Kehoe, Thomas F. "The Boarding School Bison Drive Site." *Plains Anthropologist,* Memoir 4, vol. 12, no. 35, 1967.

Roe, F. G. "White Buffalo." In *Proceedings and Transactions of the Royal Society of Canada,* 3d ser., vol. 38, 155–173. Ottawa, 1944.

Speth, John D. *Bison Kills and Bone Counts.* Chicago, Ill.: University of Chicago Press, 1983.

Wheat, Joe Ben. "The Olsen-Chubbock Site: A Paleo-Indian Bison Kill." *Memoirs of the Society for American Archaeology,* no. 26. Issued as *American Antiquity,* vol. 37, no. 1, pt. 2, January 1972.

CHILDREN'S BOOKS

Lepthien, Emilie U. *Buffalo.* A New True Book. Chicago, Ill.: Childrens Press, 1989.

Nicholson, John D. *The White Buffalo.* New York: Platt and Munk, 1965.

Roop, Peter. *Buffalo Jump.* Flagstaff, Ariz.: Northland Publishing, 1996.

Sample, Michael S. *Bison: Symbol of the American West.* Helena, Mont.: Falcon Press, 1987.

INDEX

Bold entries indicate photographs or drawings